KU-344-340

Dryden – On Counselling

Volume 2: A Dialogue

Windy Dryden

and

Antonio Branco Vasco

Foreword by Arnold A. Lazarus

W

Whurr Publishers
London and New Jersey

210234

Copyright © Windy Dryden 1991

First published 1991 by

Whurr Publishers Limited
19b Compton Terrace
London N1 2UN
England

All rights reserved. This book is protected by
copyright. No part of this book may be reproduced
in any form or by any means, including
photocopying, or utilised by any information storage
or retrieval system without written permission from
the copyright owner.

British Library Cataloguing in Publication Data
Dryden, Windy
    Dryden on counselling: Vol 2. A dialogue.
    I. Title   II.   Vasco, Antonio Branco
    361.3

    ISBN 1-870332-67-9

Phototypeset by Scribe Design, Gillingham, Kent
Printed in Great Britain by Athenaeum Press Ltd,
Newcastle upon Tyne

Foreword

Windy Dryden, at the tender age of 41, has his name on the cover of 39 books (as author, co-author, editor or co-editor). He has not sacrificed quality for quantity, and professional reviews of his works have been uniformly positive. The present book provides clues about his drive, his motivation and his ability to be so prolific. We also learn some of the major ideas he espouses after immersing himself so deeply in the areas of counselling and therapy. It is rare to pin someone down who is always on the go and who is so productive. How nice to be able to sit and chat about really significant ideas and interpersonal events, and tap into an expert's pool of wisdom and experience. Antonio Branco Vasco has accomplished the foregoing quite admirably.

Stimulating, and at times provocative, remarks on theory, research, practice and training abound. Personally, I am eager to use this book in my seminars and classes because I feel sure that it will generate active, lively and meaningful debates. There is much to be learned from Dryden's insights and reflections. People who are themselves thinking about consulting someone for counselling or psychotherapy might profit from perusing Chapter 5 in which Dr Dryden points to ever-present pitfalls and traps to be avoided.

The issues that struck me as most open to debate concern Dr Dryden's remarks about client deterioration, or what is also called 'negative outcome'. For instance, he is strongly opposed to forming friendships with clients, or getting them to do jobs in return for payment, because such 'over-involvement' may undermine treatment. Yet a few of my former clients have become very good friends of mine, and I see nothing wrong with a 'barter system' in some instances. True, there are specific patient characteristics associated with a higher risk for negative outcome, and it behoves counsellors and therapists to really know their customers before intervening in untraditional ways. In this context, Dryden's personal experiences with psychoanalytical and person-centred orientations make interesting reading.

I think that most readers will enjoy the poignant and personal glimpses this book provides – it taps into many experiences, thoughts and feelings that Windy Dryden shares quite compellingly. For example, his observations about preventing counsellor burn-out are intriguing.

Basically, the dialogue between Windy Dryden and Antonio Branco Vasco provides impetus for a great deal of stimulating thought. In keeping with Dr Dryden's distaste for jargon, it is easy and pleasurable reading throughout.

Arnold A. Lazarus, PhD
Distinguished Professor
Graduate School of Applied and Professional Psychology
Rutgers – The State University of New Jersey

Preface

In this, the second volume of a three part series entitled 'Dryden on Counselling' I am interviewed by Antonio Branco Vasco, a leading Portuguese psychologist and psychotherapist. Antonio suggested this project to me while I was teaching at the University of Lisbon in the summer of 1990 and we recorded the interviews soon after my teaching commitments were over.

The intention of this project is to capture an informal discussion between two colleagues but with the focus mainly on the ideas of one of them. Chapter 1 begins with my reflections on which personal experiences influenced my decision to become a counsellor and continues with a discussion of my own experiences of personal therapy. In the second chapter I grapple with the difficult issue of the distinction between counselling and psychotherapy before outlining my ideas on service delivery. In Chapter 3 I reflect on my major contributions to rational–emotive therapy (RET), whilst in the fourth chapter I state my views on the current position concerning eclecticism and integration in counselling. Chapter 5 contains advice I often give to people who seek counselling for themselves, while in Chapter 6 I discuss client deterioration and counsellor burn-out. Finally, in Chapter 7, I consider my personal contribution to the field of counselling.

I believe that this volume, in its informal style, complements the formal exposition of the other two volumes in this series.

I wish to thank Antonia Macaro, Margaret Ledden and Jane Sugarman for their invaluable help in the preparation of the manuscript.

Windy Dryden, London
November 1990

Contents

Chapter 1
Personal Influences

Antonio Branco Vasco: What was the most important reason you became a counsellor?

Windy Dryden: I think there are a number of reasons why I became interested in counselling and psychotherapy. Let me just reflect on the main reasons, although in retrospect we can often never be sure that they were the exact reasons. But let me see if I can highlight some of the main influences.

The first influence was being an only child, and I think that was important for a number of reasons. First, I believe that being an only child meant that I really learned to interact with myself quite a lot and was able to tolerate my own company: in fact I liked my own company and always have done. I think that this is important because I learned, or we can even say taught myself, to become aware of my inner experiences. I wouldn't exactly call myself an introvert, but earlier on in my life I was certainly more introverted than I am now. Being introverted meant that I became interested in the inner life; so I think that was a major influence.

Another influence that goes along with this is the fact that my parents, although very loving — and this applies more to my mother than to my father perhaps — were somewhat over-intrusive. So, in order to maintain a sense of identity, again I needed to retreat into my own inner experience, and became quite familiar with my psychological processes.

Another important influence was the fact that I used to have a very bad stammer. I still stammer to some degree, but when I was younger it used to be much more apparent than it is now. At secondary school a lot of the boys were quite unkind, particularly in groups, where they would mimic me and criticise me, which I found very hurtful. So I became aware of hurtful inner experiences which sensitised me to the fact that human beings could experience psychological pain. This type of experience had another interesting aspect to it, in that the same boys who would get together in groups to mimic me and laugh at me were individually quite kind to me, and therefore I became interested in the influence of groups on people's behaviour. It really did fascinate me that boys who could be friendly and kind individually could become quite vicious and nasty in groups, and that is why I became interested in human behaviour. It oriented me towards psychology in general, and I think that the psychological hurt I experienced led me later on in life to want to help people who experienced similar inner pain. So those are some of the main experiences that oriented me towards counselling and psychotherapy.

Now, let me say that I was very good at languages at school and maybe, if I hadn't had a stammer, I would perhaps have decided to go on and study languages at university, but it quickly became apparent to me that having a stammer would mean that I would either just be a translator, which didn't interest me, or I would have to become involved in languages in ways that did not entail speaking. But I couldn't really see how I could make a career of this, so I quickly decided to look around for something else; I learned about the discipline of psychology and decided to study that. The psychology course which I took was a fairly good one and emphasised social rather than experimental psychology.

Antonio Branco Vasco: At what point did you consider a career in counselling?

Windy Dryden: I didn't really consider a career in counselling until I studied for my PhD, which was on the topic of self-disclosure in an experimental, social psychology situation. The more I got into this area, the more I came across references to counselling, which reawakened my interest in exploring my own psychological processes. I also got caught up with the human potential movement in the late 1960s and early 1970s, when I used to go to many encounter groups and the like. This again seemed to reinforce my interest in exploring the possibility of a career in the helping professions, but I never really thought of being just a counsellor, because I like variety in my life. I have always been quite academically minded, so when I trained as a counsellor in 1974–75 I was looking for a way of marrying my interest in the academic life to a clinical career, and luckily an opportunity presented itself to me: in 1975 I joined the lecturing staff at the University of Aston, which meant that I could actualise these two major aspects of my life – the academic and the helping – and I have been lucky enough to be able to pursue these twin aspects throughout my career so far.

Antonio Branco Vasco: Your thoughts about the relationship between your early life and your professional choice are very interesting. Do you think that people who choose a career in the helping professions have similar early experiences?

Windy Dryden: Well, I am not quite sure how general it is, although certainly the research that has been done on the personal lives of psychotherapists seems to indicate that this is an important aspect. For example, when I recently co-edited a book entitled *On Becoming a Psychotherapist* (Dryden and Spurling, 1989), the practitioners who wrote about themselves did seem to point to some early experience of psychological pain. Also, I have to select people for a training course in counselling, and I certainly think it is helpful to have some early – and how early is a matter of conjecture – experience of either being in psychological pain yourself, or being around somebody in psychological pain, say family or friends, or helping somebody in this way. I think that this is important, although it depends on what the person has made of it; a person could have experienced early psychological pain without really learning from it or moving forward, and I don't think that people who have early instances of psychological pain and become stuck in it make very good counsellors until they have dealt with that particular situation. I think that people who don't make good candidates are people who really haven't had any experience of psychological pain, either their own or other people's, and seem to have a very naïve view of what the helping professions are like – people who lack, if you like, an experiential foundation on which to draw. So I don't think early psychological pain is necessary, but I think it is often helpful in determining the individual motivation for becoming a counsellor or psychotherapist.

Antonio Branco Vasco: So it would be important to be around psychological pain. Does it have to be early in life?

Windy Dryden: No, I think it can come later in life, and we certainly have enough informal evidence now that people who have, for example, experienced the loss of a child or some other loss become interested in helping other people in similar situations, as a way perhaps of repairing the hurt. Now, this can be problematic, because although I think this is a healthy motivation, if it becomes a crusade, and I think it *can* become a crusade, then it is potentially dangerous. So I think later experience of psychological pain or actually helping others can also be quite productive, so long as it doesn't become, as I say, a crusade.

Antonio Branco Vasco: Can you be more explicit about the idea of a crusade; do you mean people becoming too self-centred?

Windy Dryden: Right! It's as if that crusade becomes the raison d'être of the person's life at that time. Everything else becomes subordinated to it, and his or her entire life seems to be devoted to, say, getting involved in a charity to help raise money for reducing the chances of, for example, sudden infant death syndrome. Now, on its own this is a good motivation, but when it becomes the be all and end all of a person's life, then this is problematic, because I think it is important as a counsellor and psychotherapist to find some way of getting involved in other things – other aspects of life, other interests. So I think the crusading aspect of making good the early or later hurts seems to me to be a problematic motivation for becoming a counsellor or psychotherapist.

Antonio Branco Vasco: So, going back to your life, how did you manage to find your way through the jungle of psychotherapy approaches? As you know there are about 500 such models. What were your guidelines in choosing a perspective from which to practise psychotherapy?

Windy Dryden: The issue of the choice of orientation is one that I find fascinating, because I think it probably includes personal factors – what you bring as a person to your choice of orientation – but it is also largely determined by where you happen to seek training, who happen to be your trainers and what other options seem to be available at the time. It also depends on how far you are prepared to make sacrifices, as I did, and pay out of your own pocket to obtain the training that you really think is going to be helpful to you and your clients. So let me say a little bit about that.

I was initially trained at the University of Aston in Birmingham, which at that time was still heavily influenced by the work of Carl Rogers and, although the trainer — whose name was Richard Nelson-Jones — was beginning to develop his own ideas, he and the Fulbright scholars (Aston had a number of American Fulbright professors) were still oriented towards what is now known as the person-centred approach. I was trained in this approach and I found that there were two important aspects to it which are relevant to the question that you have asked me. First of all, I found that this approach did not really fit in that well with my own personality and problem-solving style. Secondly, I found that it took clients only so far, and a number of my clients seemed to want more from me than I was actually offering them. I was offering them the basic core conditions, but they seemed to want a more specific direction in tackling their problems; so I looked around for alternatives. Now, this is where I will talk about the influence of what's available, because the only thing available at that time in Birmingham was a psychoanalytical training course, which was held at the Uffculme Clinic. I involved myself in the course there, but never really felt congruent with the psychoanalytical approach; in fact I felt less congruent with it than with the person-centred approach.

It was around 1977 that I became aware of rational–emotive therapy (RET) and fortuitously went to a workshop run by Maxie Maultsby, who pioneered a similar approach, known as rational behaviour therapy. I then met up with an Englishman called Stephen Flett, who had a long-standing interest in rational–emotive therapy and who arranged for a woman called Virginia Anne Church to come over from the States to run a 5-day workshop, which I attended. That workshop really stimulated my interest, and it was there that I realised that in order for me to get a rigorous training in rational–emotive therapy I would have to go to the USA, since there were no opportunities to train in RET in Britain at that time. I therefore went to America — at some personal financial cost, I should add — and found that RET seemed to be offering what I was looking for — a much more structured and, from the client's point of view, more helpful way of tackling personal problems.

Antonio Branco Vasco: I think that is an important point. You have discussed the person-centred approach to therapy, in which some of the qualities of the relationship are authenticity and congruence, so I would infer from what you say that you think it is important for there to be congruence between your personality style and the kind of therapy you practise.

Windy Dryden: I think that's important, but I also think that there is a hidden danger there: that is, your style also has to be congruent with the client's epistemology and approach to personal problem-solving; therefore I think that, as counsellors and psychotherapists, we always have to be on our guard against assuming that, because we as individuals find this particular approach suited to our style and helpful to us personally – as rational–emotive therapy was and still is to me – therefore it is going to be helpful to all our clients. This is a danger.

Antonio Branco Vasco: If you think that this is a danger, would you argue that it is important to think both about the client's problem and about the client's personality style before accepting him or her for therapy?

Windy Dryden: Yes, and in an ideal world we would have a situation similar to the old institution of the matchmaker – you would go and see her if you wanted to get married and she would have a wide knowledge of the people available in your community and, through that knowledge, could match you with a particular potential mate, somebody who was right for you. Now, as I say, in an ideal world we would have a kind of therapeutic matchmaker who, through interviewing you and knowing the vast resources in the community (now I realise that a lot of communities don't have vast resources, but let me just pursue this analogy for a moment), would match you with a therapist who was just right for *you*. I think that would be the ideal, but we are far from it; therefore counsellors need to be flexible in their therapeutic approach and tailor it as far as they can to the client they have before them – although there are of course limits as to how much a particular therapist can range between the different epistemologies that underlie different approaches.

Antonio Branco Vasco: Was your choice of rational–emotive therapy just a theoretical one or did it have anything to do with your experiences as a client?

Windy Dryden: Well, yes, I have been a client in four different formal therapies. I say formal because, as I mentioned earlier, I went to many encounter groups in my early twenties and also, in my mid-twenties, I was involved with the re-evaluation co-counselling movement, which is more of an informal counselling network. But let me just talk about my four experiences as a client, because I think I am reasonably unique, in that I am involved in counselling but have never had a very productive experience of being a client, and I think that this has probably led me to be ambivalent about advising my trainees to become clients themselves.

My first experience of being a client was while I was training to be a counsellor at Aston University. Around that time I had become aware of being mildly to moderately depressed, lethargic and somewhat less active than I normally am. I ended up with a therapist who had been recommended to me in London – I used to go home at weekends – and who turned out to be influenced by the work of Melanie Klein which I didn't know about at that time. He seemed to be a kindly man, but I really found it very difficult to use the kind of therapy that he was practising. For example, I would talk quite a lot, in a very unstructured way, about my thoughts, feelings and experiences, which I found – and still find – helpful, but I was looking for something to help me with my depression and, every time I asked him for more help than he was giving me, he would interpret that as a wish that I had for him to 'feed' me. I still have a vivid image in my mind of him taking his hands away from his face – he seemed to have them in front of his face most of the time, as I recall – slightly rocking forward, then saying, 'Windy, I think you again want me to feed you', then going back, placing his hands in front of his face and retreating into silence. Now, I found that difficult to cope with and didn't quite understand what to make of it. Around that time I moved my home to Birmingham and decided as a result to terminate therapy. I suppose I could have gone back to London every week to continue it as I had done previously, but it wasn't helping me that much, although I wonder even now what would have happened if I had persisted with it. But I didn't in general find it that helpful, other than as an opportunity to explore my thoughts, feelings and experiences in an unstructured way.

I then went to consult a psychiatrist who had taught at the University of Aston – I was, you could say, a student of his – and again he was a kindly man whom I saw weekly in the context of the National Health Service, again I guess for about 2 or 3 months. Now, that was an interesting experience, because what I recall from it is that he started off somewhat psychoanalytically oriented and took a lot of notes while I was talking. He was flexible, however, because when I pointed out that I found his note-taking very off-putting, he stopped it. He also used some psychodrama techniques with me, where I would play the roles of significant others in my life and use the empty chair technique, and I found that much more helpful as a client than a more passive approach to therapy. I also still have a fairly vivid image of the two of us smoking cigars – I jokingly say that his cigar was larger than my cigar, and no doubt Siggie Freud would have something to say about that!! Anyway, I found these more active techniques somewhat helpful and, although they didn't help me over my depression, I did find that I was more inclined to be active as a client. He then got an academic job at the University of Birmingham and had to wind down with all his NHS clients, and as a result arranged for me to see somebody in the same clinic.

This experience was also very interesting, because I learned quite a lot about what *not* to do as a therapist from this guy. He was a much more traditional Freudian – somewhat cold, not kindly like the other two therapists, and used to spend quite a bit of time staring out of the window. Again I couldn't make head or tail of this, and when I asked whether he was doing this to facilitate the transference, I remember him laughing in what seemed to me to be a fairly mocking way. One of the things that I still remember to this day, and I think it was quite helpful in the long run, although not by design, is him saying to me – very unexpectedly, because we hadn't discussed the length of therapy – that this was going to be our last session. I said, 'What can I do?' and he said 'Well, you could continue to see me in my private practice if you wanted to'. I was pretty annoyed and somewhat hurt about this, and realised at this point that if I wanted some help I had better damn well help myself.

This was again at the time when I was beginning to get interested in rational–emotive therapy. I read *A New Guide to Rational Living* (Ellis and Harper, 1975) and realised quite quickly that I was depressed because I was condemning myself. Now the interesting thing is that none of the previous three therapies had really highlighted the fact that I was putting myself down, demanding that I *should* be more effective than I was and issues such as this, and through reading *A New Guide to Rational Living* I was helped to see what I could do about it. So I got the advice that I was looking for from therapy from a book!! That led me to put it into practice and, within a fairly short order, I learned how to deal with my depression and to become relatively undepressed.

Antonio Branco Vasco: Had you previously had any experiences of helping yourself with your problems?

Windy Dryden: Yes. That experience is similar to how I helped myself get over my stammer. I had been referred to several speech therapists and hadn't got much help from them at all. The most help I got was from an informal speech therapist who taught me how to speak 'on the breath', and listened to me read and things like that. At the same time I remember listening to a radio programme on which a well-known English comedian, Michael Bentine, said that he overcame his stammer by adopting the attitude that if he stammered he stammered, too bad. That sounded like good advice, so I decided to put it into practice and I said to myself, a little more vigorously than he did, 'If I stammer, I stammer – Fuck it!', therefore anticipating one of the most important techniques of RET – how to dispute your irrational beliefs vigorously. But then I also acted; I took this attitude into situations and resolved to speak up, although for a time I really got worse rather than better, but I persisted and persisted and persisted, and what happened was that I became less anxious about speaking up and, if you become less anxious about stammering, you stammer less. So, looking back on it, that experience seems to be congruent again with the interest I was developing in rational–emotive therapy, and it really showed me that I, and presumably other people, could really go a long way with self-help. What is often lacking is really a fairly consistent, if you like, education on how we make ourselves anxious and depressed and what we can do about overcoming these feelings.

So I brought to RET a personal experience of self-help and an awareness of how we can change our feelings, as well as an interest in people's attitudes, which had probably been fostered by my experiences at school. I realised that RET could bring the various strands of my life together, and that through it I could help myself and my clients. I have been practising rational–emotive therapy ever since, although I have other therapeutic interests, and the work of Ellis and his colleagues is not the only influence on my therapeutic practice.

Antonio Branco Vasco: Have you had any recent experience of being a client?

Windy Dryden: Recently I decided to go back into therapy, not because I was in any pain or anything, but for three main reasons. The first was that I was advising my trainees at Goldsmiths' College to go into therapy, and therefore I thought I would take my own advice; the second was that I wanted to test out my hypothesis and see whether I could be helped in psychotherapy as a client, and the third was that I was coming up to the age of 40 and thought that going along to a Jungian therapist might be helpful because Jung seemed to specialise in issues of that age. I only went for about five or six sessions and it seemed to me that, again, I found the opportunity to reflect out loud quite helpful, but when the therapist made any interventions it was quite clear that her views on therapy and emotions were almost in direct contradiction to mine. Again she seemed like a nice woman, but I decided that I wasn't going to spend a large amount of money on it, and so what I do now is every once in a while I take a tape recorder, go into my room on my own and talk aloud. I find it helpful to interact with myself, and I can replay the tape if I want to.

Those are some of my major experiences in terms of psychotherapy. Three of those therapists were OK on the core conditions – even the Kleinian was kind! But the third therapist, the Freudian exuded coldness and detachment, and I don't think that was helpful – I don't advocate these qualities in therapy. But it taught me that it is important to seek the kind of therapy that is congruent with your own particular learning style. Even though the second of these therapists was somewhat flexible, his range of flexibility didn't seem to encompass what I wanted him to offer. So what I have learned from all this is that, when a client requires the kind of help that is beyond my expertise, then I will refer him or her to somebody who is more likely to to be able to help. I think that one of the hallmarks of a good therapist is being able to refer – not to believe that you have to help everybody.

Antonio Branco Vasco: So, did your matchmakings lead you to become your own therapist?

Windy Dryden: That's right. I went to myself as matchmaker and realised that I was my own best therapist, with a little help from Ellis's writings and the Michael Bentine incident. I seem to be a fairly independently minded person, therefore I am drawn to therapies that encourage people to utilise whatever resources they have to help themselves.

Antonio Branco Vasco: Have you ever been a client in RET?

Windy Dryden: Well, that's an interesting question, and the answer is yes and no. Not for any extended period of time, but in the course of my visits to Albert Ellis, which have taken place regularly ever since 1978, he has made time freely available for me in his lunch and supper-time sessions to discuss various professional matters, and on two or three occasions I have brought up personal issues that I couldn't help myself with. I guess you could say I was really going to him as a consultant rather than as a therapist. He worked too fast for me, but once I had slowed him down – maybe he thought that since I was very much into RET I could work at his pace – I found that he was able to spot some very subtle irrational beliefs that I wasn't aware of and, as soon as I would become aware of one, I would know what to do about it. So I have had that limited experience of being an RET client.

Antonio Branco Vasco: And does Albert Ellis's therapeutic style match your personality style as a client?

Windy Dryden: Well, now it does, but it would have been interesting to see whether it would have when I was first going to therapy in my mid-twenties. Looking back I think that what I did appreciate in those therapists was their kindness, and I don't know whether I would have got that degree of kindness from Albert if I had gone to him off the street. However, when I went to him we shared a knowledge of an interest in RET, and since then he has been very kind to me over the years.

Antonio Branco Vasco: Thank you Windy.

Chapter 2
Service Delivery

Antonio Branco Vasco: I would like to hear your views on the differences and similarities between counselling and psychotherapy.

Windy Dryden: Well, my view is that there is no substantial difference, that the two terms exist for reasons other than definite distinctions between the two activities. Given this view I will use the term 'counselling' more frequently than the term 'psychotherapy' throughout this book.

I think that if I was going to make a distinction between them, I would say that counselling was a shorter-term intervention with clients who were less severely disturbed; and that psychotherapy was a longer-term intervention with people who were more severely disturbed. But in terms of activities – whether we would be able to distinguish counselling activities from psychotherapy activities – I would be hard put to come up with real differences. I am aware, however, that many people do make distinctions between counselling and psychotherapy. The psychoanalytical community definitely does, and therapists within that community also make distinctions between psychotherapy and psychoanalysis. But the activities that I do wouldn't fit their criteria of counselling, because they define counselling as a much more supportive activity than psychotherapy, in which you don't work on underlying issues, you don't confront defences and so on. Even my own distinction, which is in terms of the population seen and the time spent with clients, is problematic, because people who call themselves counsellors do long-term work with people who are very disturbed. Would we say that they are doing counselling or psychotherapy? Another issue is that the expressions 'short-term therapy' and 'long-term counselling' have become current in the literature. Well, what's the difference? Now, if we were to answer the question empirically, we would take tapes from people who call themselves psychotherapists and tapes from people who call themselves counsellors and see if any differences emerged from what they actually did. A study like this would be interesting because it could help to broaden the debate, but I am quite sceptical about the chance of finding any real differences.

There are reasons other than clear distinctions between the activities for the existence of the two terms. Counselling is much less threatening a term than psychotherapy, and therefore perhaps more acceptable in contexts such as student counselling services in Britain. I don't think you would have got too many student psychotherapy services, so there are issues of acceptability. There are also issues of status. Some people would be quite insulted if you called them counsellors – they see themselves as psychotherapists because it is a 'deeper and more specialised activity'. Well, that's got less to do with the actual activities than with sociological considerations of status. So I am happy to call myself a counsellor, a psychotherapist or whatever, because I don't think it's going to influence what I do.

Antonio Branco Vasco: So you would agree with the statement that psychotherapists do what counsellors call counselling and counsellors do what psychotherapists call psychotherapy?

Windy Dryden: If the study I mentioned earlier were to be carried out, I would not be surprised to find that it would produce such an outcome.

Antonio Branco Vasco: You didn't mention that another commonly held feature of counselling is that it is supposed to deal with normal life crises, rather than with psychological disturbance.

Windy Dryden: That's right, but I think it was implicit in my definition. Why would people who are relatively undisturbed go and see a counsellor other than because of lifespan developmental crises? But you are right to make that explicit.

Antonio Branco Vasco: Do you think there should be a distinction between counselling and psychotherapy training courses?

Windy Dryden: Well, not if we are talking about professional counselling as opposed to using counselling skills in the context of another discipline or profession. The British Association for Counselling draws a distinction between professional counsellors and other helping professionals, such as social workers or nurses, who use counselling skills in their work. That is quite a clear distinction, because if you only want to use counselling skills in your work there are probably a whole host of subjects you don't really need to study on a training course.

But if we restrict our discussion to psychotherapists and professional counsellors, then I don't think there is a need for widely different types of training. And that logically follows from my own failure to come up with a definition that clearly discriminates between the two activities. So, whether I was training counsellors or psychotherapists, I would include theory, skills, workshops, supervision, and some type of personal development group where trainees can explore their relationships with each other. In addition, although again I am ambivalent about this, I would recommend some degree of personal therapy. I think that these strands are necessary for both psychotherapists and counsellors.

Antonio Branco Vasco: What about the importance of psychopathology and the nosographic classifications?

Windy Dryden: That would come under the academic component, together with the issues of diagnosis and psychiatry.

Antonio Branco Vasco: So you think that it would be important for both counsellors and psychotherapists to learn something about psychopathology and nosographic classifications?

Windy Dryden: Yes, I would probably include in a training course some of the basic research that has been done on anxiety, depression and other forms of emotional disturbance, as well as some information on diagnostic systems. This is not because I would encourage counsellors or therapists to use these systems themselves, since I think they can be problematic, but because they should be familiar with the work of other professionals, such as psychiatrists, and with the professional constructs these other groups use. But I would not necessarily want to teach them about diagnostic classification systems so that they use them themselves.

Antonio Branco Vasco: What importance do you attach to nosographic classifications as a tool in clinical decision-making?

Windy Dryden: Well, there are advantages and disadvantages. Let's take something that is currently in vogue – borderline personality disorder. The advantages of using such a classification is that you can look up the research and writings on that subject in the literature and be reasonably certain that the researchers and writers are all talking about the same thing. Therefore you can pick up some helpful hints about the likely responses of such clients and modify your approach accordingly. The problem is that for this particular person, who is with you at this particular time, that may not be enough, because what is productive for one person with borderline personality disorder may not be appropriate for someone else who has been given the same diagnosis. So I wouldn't like to encourage the use of these classifications if it meant treating people uniformly just because they have a particular personality disorder. A classification can be helpful by providing guidelines and introducing some clarity into the literature, but it can also be problematic if it leads to minimising individual differences. Hans Eysenck (1990), in his recent autobiography, made that point by saying that within any psychiatric classification system the concept of individual differences must never be forgotten. So I think that classifications can be useful tools, but they should not be used too simplistically.

Antonio Branco Vasco: So would you give more weight to personal characteristics than to psychiatric classifications?

Windy Dryden: Yes, and I find it very interesting that American *psychologists* seem to have bought hook, line and sinker the DSM-III(R) system. There has been discussion in the American Psychological Association about moving towards a classification system based on empirical psychological research, but I haven't seen that discussed recently, so I don't know whether they have dropped it. We should be aware of the advantages and disadvantages of using these systems.

Antonio Branco Vasco: Are you personally comfortable with the term 'counselling' or do you think it sounds too much like advice-giving?

Windy Dryden: Well, that's an interesting point, because the word counselling has a much broader meaning than it has within psychotherapeutic traditions, and we cannot legitimately claim the word as our own and restrict its meaning. In other fields the word 'counselling' means to take control or to give advice. Although quite a few counsellors really don't find the concept of advice-giving very productive, there is some research which shows that advice-giving can be therapeutic, not so much because the person follows your advice, but because they start thinking about it. It has a stimulating effect. So I am not uncomfortable with the term 'counselling' in view of those connotations, because I don't rule out advice-giving at all as part of counselling or psychotherapy. You can overdo it, as you can overdo anything, but it certainly has its place. I wouldn't like to think that being a counsellor prevents me from giving advice, as some counsellors would have it.

Antonio Branco Vasco: Do you have any examples of productive advice-giving?

Windy Dryden: I quite often use it as part of self-disclosure, saying such things as, 'Well I remember, when I was in a situation similar to yours, I considered this. Does that make any sense to you? Would you follow that course of action for yourself?', and the person might say 'No, but something similar has just come to mind which I could possibly consider'. I certainly would not advocate advice-giving if it meant coming across as saying, 'You must do this because I am the great expert and I have determined that this is what you have to do'. However, I think that discussion of alternatives and the pros and cons of alternatives, as a way of stimulating somebody, is fine.

Antonio Branco Vasco: The literature doesn't show any outcome differences between individual therapy, group therapy, family therapy and so on. What is your view on the usefulness of different modalities in psychotherapy?

Windy Dryden: What you call modalities I have called in the past therapeutic arenas (Dryden, 1984a). I think there needs to be a lot more research on this issue, because the research that has been done hasn't covered all orientations. So we need to investigate the therapeutic value of arenas, including orientations, as an independent variable. This is where my interest in what is called the working alliance or the therapeutic alliance becomes particularly salient. What I think is important in working with a client is choosing an arena that will maximise the therapeutic impact and foster an effective therapeutic alliance.

I must mention here that I rarely, if ever, work with families. I haven't been trained to work with families, I certainly haven't been trained to work with children and family therapy is most often used when children are involved. I work with couples, with individuals and I *can* work with groups, but the settings in which I work make group therapy difficult to organise. I certainly don't have the facilities for group therapy in my private practice, and convening a group in the context of the National Health Service, where I do some of my work, is also difficult as a result of the clients' lifestyle and their reserve in talking about their problems to strangers who aren't professionals.

Group therapy does save a lot of therapeutic time, and research shows that you don't lose in effectiveness what you gain in time, but if clients don't want to go to a group, you can't make them. Therefore going back to the issue of therapeutic arenas, one of the major considerations in my clinical decision-making is whether clients can see the therapeutic value of working in a particular arena. If they can't, even after I have explained the rationale for my suggestion, then there would be no value in trying to force them.

Antonio Branco Vasco: That means that clients' decision-making processes are as important as therapists' decision-making processes.

Windy Dryden: That's a very good point, because we often talk about clinical decision-making processes in isolation, and in counselling it is certainly not the case that the counsellor makes decisions and processes information in isolation from the client. A counsellor could be a first-class clinical decision-maker, but if he or she doesn't take the client's view into account, that will have a negative impact on the therapeutic process, in that the client may feel coerced into an alien arena.

Antonio Branco Vasco: You said that your experience has concentrated mainly on individual and couple counselling. Do you think there are different training needs for these two therapeutic arenas?

Windy Dryden: Yes, I do, very much so, because working with one client in the room is really quite different from working with two clients in the room. Having a threesome there tends to lead to the development of a two-against-one type of situation, if you are not careful. Therefore the ideal would be to devise a training that provided sufficient experience both in individual and in couple counselling, but this may be impossible due to time constraints. On the course that I run, for example, which is a 3-year part-time Master's course, we don't have the time to train people up to a high level of expertise in both arenas.

The other point worth bearing in mind about training is that some people have argued that rigorous training in individual counselling may make subsequent training in couple counselling harder, in that people would get too used to working with one person – exploring the fantasies, the dreams, the inner psychological processes of that one person. Then they might find the extra drama and complexity of couple counselling difficult to master.

So, for example, in an organisation such as Relate: National Marriage Guidance, people are trained to work with couples right from the start. I think that this is right, because it is probably easier to learn to deal with one person on his or her own if you have been first trained in couple work than vice versa, although this is an empirical question.

Antonio Branco Vasco: Do you think counsellors should be allowed to work exclusively with couples or exclusively with individuals, or do you think they should have a broader spectrum?

Windy Dryden: Well, when you say 'should they be allowed', the question is who is going to stop them? But if we leave that aside for a moment, I do know lots of people who work only with individuals and, if they are in private practice, they can earn a living out of it. But I think that if you see couples you are much more likely to end up seeing individuals as well, because it frequently happens that one of the partners drops out in mid-counselling and, unless you take the stance that you will only see the couple together, which I think has its difficulties, then you are bound to see individuals. Anyway, in Britain we certainly don't have a comprehensive training that covers thoroughly all four arenas (individual, couple, family and group); therefore, again I think that a practitioner should have a referral network. If you are not comfortable about or skilled in seeing couples or families, refer them to a practitioner who is.

Antonio Branco Vasco: Do you think that if a counsellor becomes an expert in one of the arenas, he or she will be more efficient than others who cover more than one?

Windy Dryden: Probably yes, although the issue of counsellor skill is the one gaping hole in the whole arena of counselling and psychotherapy research. Again this is an empirical question, but it hasn't received much attention until recently, so we have to wait for research results.

Antonio Branco Vasco: What are your personal preferences in terms of arenas?

Windy Dryden: I mentioned earlier that I haven't worked in the arena of family counselling. I have reflected on why that is and, apart from the fact that I think you really would need to specialise in child psychology and psychopathology to work effectively in family counselling, I think it may again be related to my being an only child. My hypothesis is that, since being an only child for me entailed spending a fair amount of productive time alone, I would not find the complexity and the chaotic aspects of family work to my taste. I don't think I will ever get around to testing this hypothesis, because I can't see myself getting involved in family counselling in the future. But I am quite comfortable in either couple or individual work. Now that I have developed a particular approach to couple counselling that seems to be quite helpful to my clients, I don't find it at all chaotic, although I know that some people who go into couple work, after being trained in individual counselling, do find it chaotic.

I have enjoyed group counselling whenever I have practised it, because you can encourage people to be 'helpful' as well as 'helped' and that is a very important therapeutic factor. I remember that many years ago, while I was at the University of Aston, I was seeing a male student in individual counselling who was making slow, but reasonable, progress. Then he joined a group I had set up and started making great leaps and bounds forwards. When we talked about it later, we identified two curative group factors that were lacking in individual counselling. One was the notion of universality: he found it enormously helpful to discover that other people had similar problems to him and that he wasn't the freak he thought he was. I had pointed this out to him many times, but it wasn't the same as the experience of him actually seeing it and hearing other people talking about their problems. The other factor that he found therapeutic was learning that he could be helpful to others. Now, unless the individual counsellor allows the client to help him or her, which is problematic, the individual client will not have a comparable experience.

Antonio Branco Vasco: Wouldn't you say that group counselling is even more chaotic than family counselling?

Windy Dryden: Not in my experience, because the participants in group work are all strangers to one another, and that is probably less chaotic than dealing with a family unit whose members know each other far better than they know you. Therefore I don't find group counselling that chaotic, and I actually enjoy it, especially when it is focused on one problem, such as examination anxiety.

Antonio Branco Vasco: You never trained in child therapy. Is that because you don't like working with children?

Windy Dryden: I like children in small doses: I am pretty good with them, although my wife says that I get involved too quickly and enthusiastically with them, and as a result either they get frightened of me or I get tired out, because I play with them too vigorously. But I have never been that interested in child psychology or psychopathology. I find children interesting, but I think I would make a much better uncle than a father, because as an uncle you can play with the kids for about half an hour and then go home, but if you are a father you can't go home – although you can *leave* home! So that has never really interested me.

Antonio Branco Vasco: Why do you think you became interested in couple counselling?

Windy Dryden: I became interested in it while doing some as part of my training in rational–emotive therapy in New York. I took from that training the idea of helping people to overcome their individual disturbances before tackling their dissatisfactions with the relationship, because trying to get people to communicate or negotiate when they are anxious, depressed or very angry with each other is generally uesless in the long term.

So in a chapter that I wrote in the mid-1980s called 'Marital therapy: the rational–emotive approach' (Dryden, 1985a), I formulated this idea much more clearly than I had ever seen it formulated before and this helped me to make sense of a potentially problematic process. I think that as a couple counsellor you must be more active and directive than you need to be as an individual counsellor, because if you are not, then the couples are likely to argue or refuse to talk, therefore, you need to be quite creative too.

When I was living in Birmingham in the early 1980s, I learned that the local Marriage Guidance Council had long waiting lists. One of the things I consider to be really criminal is providing a service and having long waiting lists. We need to respond to waiting lists quickly and with creativity. So I volunteered my services and they made me go through their training programme, which helped me to become part of that particular organisation, although it wasn't that helpful in and of itself. Doing voluntary counselling has always been quite important to me, so I decided to use my developing ideas on couple counselling in a situation where I could also fulfil my desire to be helpful in a voluntary capacity. I discovered that I enjoyed it and that I was also pretty good at it, so I have been doing it on and off ever since.

Antonio Branco Vasco: What changes would you like to see in service delivery provision in counselling in Britain?

Windy Dryden: Well, I have an ideal, although in Britain we are miles away from it. I would like to see some kind of national counselling service that could provide practitioners from different orientations, and experts in different arenas. It wouldn't be enough to be referred to a family counsellor, because the people involved may be suited to, say, psychoanalytical rather than behavioural family work and, however integrative and eclectic people try to be, it is difficult to think of an amalgam between these two.

So I would like to see a service employing people of different genders, different ethnic backgrounds, different ages, and different areas of expertise and orientations – from integrative or eclectic to more specialised ones. A client, for example, may be assigned a black counsellor, from a client-centred orienta- tion, skilled at couple counselling because it had been discovered from an intake interview that this was the exact type of help suitable to this client.

What happens at the moment leaves a lot to be desired, even if we forget about the ideal situation. One of the problems with individual counselling services, for example, is that they tend to be staffed by similar, like-minded people who practise the same orientation. This problem would be overcome if healthy respect existed between different orientations – say the psychoanalytical and behavioural coummunities – and they felt free to refer to each other. This rarely happens in Britain at present. So if I were referred to an NHS clinic that just practised psychoanalytical therapy, and felt it was not the right approach for me, I would then probably be forced into the private sector. And even that would by no means guarantee that I would find the right person to help me. I may have to interview and be interviewed by quite a number of different counsellors until I found the person I was looking for – if in fact I knew what I was looking for. People may have to be helped to know what they are looking for.

So my ideas about service delivery could be summed up in one word: diversity. But at the moment sameness and uniformity seem to be the names of the game, rather than diversity.

Antonio Branco Vasco: Do you think services should have *vignettes* describing different types of counselling, so that clients can read them and choose accordingly?

Windy Dryden: Yes, indeed. There is clear research evidence showing that, if people are given descriptions or illustrations of different therapies and are then allowed to choose, it is quite likely that they will have a better outcome than if they are randomly assigned to any particular therapy or denied the therapy of their choice (Devine and Fernald, 1973). So the idea definitely makes sense. But again such an approach would be based on a model of service delivery that emphasises diversity rather than uniformity.

Chapter 3
Major Contributions
to Rational–Emotive
Therapy

Antonio Branco Vasco: What would you identify as your main contributions to the development of rational–emotive therapy?

Windy Dryden: Well, I think I have made perhaps three main contributions to RET, and I hope they have had some impact on rational–emotive therapists in general, although that would be difficult to assess. Let me say at the outset that I have not invented any of these concepts, but I have probably been responsible for making them clearer and more systematic.

The first contribution is a clearer explication of the rational–emotive treatment sequence; the second is the systematisation of what I have called 'vivid' methods in rational–emotive therapy, and the third is the application of working alliance theory, or therapeutic alliance theory, to the practice of RET. Let me consider them one at a time. Let us take the systematisation of the rational–emotive treatment sequence first.

For many years I have known that therapists new to rational–emotive therapy were given a pretty good introduction to the practice of RET through demonstration sessions by Albert Ellis or some other trainer, including myself. This is important, because if you don't have a good model it is difficult to begin to practise RET yourself. But what I noticed over the years was that people were somehow missing the subtleties and nuances of RET, and that the skills that made up the rational–emotive treatment sequence really needed to be broken down and made clear. Therefore, with the help of Raymond DiGiuseppe, I developed the 13-step rational–emotive treatment sequence, which spells out the steps you need to take in order to help somebody with a given problem. I think this is one major contribution that I have made to the RET field.

Antonio Branco Vasco: Do you think it is important to be explicit in order to help people to learn better?

Windy Dryden: Yes. The research carried out on the training of counsellors and psychotherapists shows that it is important not only to have a model to observe but also to have somebody to 'cue' you into the model, to help you to understand how the model uses a particular framework, so that you can see interventions that you would have otherwise missed. And that is what I think we have done in the primer in which the sequence is set out (Dryden and DiGiuseppe, 1990).

Antonio Branco Vasco: So you would be teaching a way of looking at therapy and knowing why you are making a decision at any given point.

Windy Dryden: That's right. Some people ask whether we always use the same sequence and the answer to that question is no. It is a helpful guide and framework and, whilst it is important to see it as such, it shouldn't be used too rigidly. As my good friend Arnold Lazarus has said on occasions: beware of the terms 'always' and 'never' in psychotherapy. One of the problems in the field of counselling and psychotherapy is that people take good flexible ideas and then make them rigid. For example, in RET it is frequently important to help people understand how their thoughts lead to their feelings before you dispute their irrational ideas, but there may be some rare occurrences where you would want to get straight into disputing irrational thoughts before helping clients to understand this connection.

Antonio Branco Vasco: Can you give me an example?

Windy Dryden: Well somebody might come to you in a very acute suicidal crisis, and you might want to help them by showing them that it would be therapeutic if they very strongly told themselves something rational. It would probably help them more if they understood first that thoughts lead to feelings, but you may not have time to do that in a crisis situation. So although it might not be a preferred practice, it is important to be flexible and respond according to the situation you find yourself in, rather than according to a favoured framework or idea.

Antonio Branco Vasco: So, you throw away the manual rather than the client?

Windy Dryden: Well, hopefully you don't throw anything away, but your major allegiance is to your client rather than to ideas. An apocryphal story which has gone around tells of a trainee psychoanalyst who said, 'the beauty about psychoanalysis is that even though the client isn't improving, at least you have the comfort of knowing that *you* are doing the right thing'. I am against this kind of philosophy in counselling. A framework is best used as a guide to good practice, not to prescribe good practice.

Antonio Branco Vasco: So, your first contribution emphasises explicitness and flexibility in RET. What about the second contribution?

Windy Dryden: The second contribution concerns what I have called vivid methods in rational—emotive therapy. There are standard ways of working with somebody in the RET treatment sequence, involving various tasks such as helping them to assess their problem, disputing their irrational ideas and so on. It is important to learn these methods.

But sometimes it is also important to put a concept in a way that is memorable for a client. Therefore I have invented some techniques of my own, collected others that were described here and there in the RET literature, and brought them together under the heading 'vivid methods in rational—emotive therapy'. I strongly believe that people are more likely to put ideas into practice outside therapy to the extent that they can remember them, and therefore one of the tasks of the counsellor, no matter what approach he or she employs, is to encourage people to remember ideas.

Some people say, for example, that they take away the image of their counsellor and at times of distress conjure it up and imagine what that person would say to them. That is a way of deliberately bringing to mind the therapeutic process. On occasions, people have told me that they had remembered some concept that I had explained or some active demonstration that I had performed because it was put in a vivid way.

People also ask whether I always use this method, and

whether my practice is full of this stuff, and the answer is no, because whilst, on the one hand, I don't think it's good to make RET a very dry, tedious process, on the other hand, you don't want to make it too much of an entertainment, or a circus sideshow. So I think that it is a good idea to keep these methods in mind and use them when they seem likely to be helpful with a given client at a given time, tailoring them to that particular client rather than applying them indiscriminately.

There is a danger with this. Once I wrote about how I threw myself to the floor and barked like a dog to teach the client vividly, experientially if you like, the difference between acting stupidly and being stupid (Dryden, 1984b). Now, I don't do that in every session by any means, and probably don't even do it with most of my clients. The trouble with putting forward a concept in writing is that people get the wrong idea that it typifies the whole of your practice.

So when you make innovations, systematise or advocate a concept, it's important to be aware that some people may misunderstand you and attribute to you a frequency of use of that concept which is unwarranted.

Antonio Branco Vasco: Do you remember what made you bark like a dog in the case you mentioned?

Windy Dryden: Well, I was probably having a tough time getting through to that client at the time I wanted to illustrate the distinction between behaviour and self, and I may have tried to do that in different ways. I may have remembered that the client had a dog – I am not sure whether this was the case – and utilised that particular situation to teach her that concept.

I should hasten to add that it is important to have developed a fairly strong therapeutic alliance, which we will discuss in a minute, before you employ some of these vivid methods. Don't run away with the notion that a new client comes in and 2 minutes later I am barking like a dog. If that ever happens it will probably be time for me to retire. All these 'flashy' techniques have their strengths, but they also have their potential dangers and weaknesses, and the more you can do them within the context of a strong therapeutic alliance, the better.

Antonio Branco Vasco: I understand that a client of yours once called you Dr Hilarious. How do you think that fits in with a vivid way of practising rational–emotive therapy?

Windy Dryden: Well, I think that the most vivid and memorable interventions that you can make are humorous ones. I think I have a pretty good sense of humour, both inside and outside counselling, and I think it is quite appropriate to use it. If you accept Ellis's point that one way of conceptualising emotional disturbance is taking yourself, others and the world *too* seriously, then encouraging people to take a comical and ironic view of themselves can be quite helpful.

The client you are referring to did have a good sense of humour, therefore I probably made what I could call a 'trial joke', a parallel, in a sense of the 'trial interpretation' in the psychoanalytical literature. I saw that she responded humorously and seemed to benefit from it. Therefore, I emphasised that dimension with her; I think it was her boyfriend who actually penned the name Dr Hilarious and then she took it on board.

But I want to add that, to quite large numbers of clients, I am Dr Serious; with other clients I am Dr Efficiency or Dr Businesslike. So again I wouldn't want anybody running away with the idea that counselling with me is like going to see a humorous film – although it could be, at times!! I emphasise humour with certain clients, but de-emphasise it with other clients.

Antonio Branco Vasco: I also understand that you like Groucho Marx. Do you make references to him in counselling?

Windy Dryden: I have probably made one or two references to Groucho Marx. Incidently, I believe that in real life he wasn't too much of an attractive personality. I wouldn't say that I use his humour because it had a 'putting-down' aspect to it. And one thing that it is important to stress is that humour is not to be directed at the person, but at what he or she thinks, says or does, in a way that clearly indicates that you as a counsellor are on his or her side. Groucho Marx's humour definitely has a dismissive and 'putting-down' quality. It is a very critical kind of humour and is thus quite probably anti-therapeutic.

Antonio Branco Vasco: Do you think it would be difficult for a person without a sense of humour to be a counsellor?

Windy Dryden: No, I think you could be a counsellor without a sense of humour. I could humorously say that you probably have to lack a sense of humour to practise some forms of therapy such as psychoanalysis, particularly if you take Freud's views that humour is quite frequently a defence. Anyway, I think that highlighting different aspects of yourself, including the humorous, at different times in the counselling process, makes for a more flexible and therefore more effective practitioner. So, yes, I think that even without humour you can be a good counsellor with some clients some of the time, but if you have humour and are prepared to use it, then you can reach more people, more of the time. However, I wouldn't recommend going overboard with it.

Antonio Branco Vasco: Your third major contribution to RET, the one I personally find most important, is your application of therapeutic alliance theory to RET. Could you say something about that?

Windy Dryden: I have already hinted at an aspect of it in my answer to your previous question, but let me expand on it. If I were to be asked which one piece of work, article, chapter in a book, or even entire book in fact, has had the most influence on me, I think I would choose an article written by Ed Bordin (1979) in which he reformulated the old concept of the working alliance – what I now call the therapeutic alliance. He broke it down into three main components: bonds, which refer to the relationship between client and counsellor and its vicissitudes; goals, which indicate that the therapeutic process is heading somewhere; and tasks, which indicate that the two participants have got things to do along that journey. I have taken that particular concept, expanded it and applied it to rational–emotive therapy.

Let me first put this into a broader context. One of the issues I have been concerned about over the years in RET is that trainees are exposed to Albert Ellis, who is certainly an excellent therapist – but it's a bit like, say, a beginner ballet dancer watching Rudolf Nureyev and trying to put what he does into practice immediately, without realising that experts do things that are based on years and years of training.

It seemed to me that in RET training the technical aspects of RET were being emphasised more than good therapeutic practice which is common to all therapies. The notion of the therapeutic alliance was a way of pointing out to RET practitioners that you can't just be good technicians to practise good RET, and that you need to be aware of good common therapeutic practice.

Another reason why I emphasise the concept of the

therapeutic alliance is that it is a good framework which can be used by counsellors interested in the field of eclecticism and integration, as I am. I really do see myself as having a broader base than rational–emotive therapy, although I have a particular 'affiliation' with it.

These were the main reasons why I adopted the concept of the alliance and applied it to RET.

Antonio Branco Vasco: What aspects of the alliance would you most like RET therapists to take note of?

Windy Dryden: That the therapist be flexible enough to tailor the interpersonal aspects of his or her therapeutic approach to the client, varying the style, emphasising one or the other of Rogers' core conditions, and focusing on either bonds or tasks according to the client being seen.

Another point that I would like RET therapists to digest is that good therapy is tailored to client's goals. Unfortunately, it is often the case, both in RET and in other therapies, that counsellors and client go off in completely different directions. Therefore it is very important to be mindful of the client's goals, although you also have to be sceptical of them, because initially they may well be influenced by the nature of the client's disturbance.

Thirdly, I would like RET practitioners to realise that both client and counsellor have tasks to perform in the process, mainly in the service of helping the client to reach his or her goals. I would again emphasise the importance of being explicit. The client needs to know what his or her tasks are, to understand how these relate to the counsellors' tasks and how carrying out these tasks will help him or her towards achieving the goals, and so on.

These issues are relevant no matter what approach to counselling you advocate, and that is what I have brought to RET. I didn't invent the concept – that was done by Ed Bordin – but I developed it, elaborated upon it, perhaps even clarified it, and made it relevant for rational–emotive therapy.

Antonio Branco Vasco: Would you say that the first thing to look at whenever you are in a situation of impasse in counselling is the quality of the therapeutic bond?

Windy Dryden: Well, not always, because you may have an ongoing sense of a good and effective bond in spite of a temporary stall.

It is, however, one of the places to look if you are considering a wide variety of factors that might help you and your client to understand why this therapeutic relationship seems to be stuck, or not going where you would hope it would go. Also, remember I am virtually always against the concept of 'always' in counselling or psychotherapy!

Antonio Branco Vasco: Do you think that the therapeutic relationship plays a more important curative role in working with clients who have so-called disorders of personality?

Windy Dryden: Yes. That domain of the alliance really needs a lot of attention with such clients because they frequently have a lot of trouble developing and maintaining cooperative relationships.

Antonio Branco Vasco: Let's move on to goals. Would you agree that it's really important to be aware of so-called hidden agendas and contradictions?

Windy Dryden: Yes. People frequently come to counselling with more than one goal, as you indicated, and these can contradict each other. The main contradiction is that clients want to get relief from their anxiety, depression or whatever, but they may not be prepared to put in the effort to overcome these problems because they have a contradictory goal of being comfortable at the moment. RET is very mindful of this particular problem.

Hidden agendas are a different matter, because by definition they are hidden, and whilst I would suggest that counsellors attend to the possibility that the client may have a so-called hidden agenda, this is difficult to identify in actuality. It can most often be inferred later on, when you have considered and dismissed other factors that could account for the client's failure to change. It could be that the client understands what he or she has to do and has the capacity to do it, that you and the client have a good relationship and that the client has a stated goal, and yet something isn't right there.

One of the things that I like doing in counselling is brainstorming with clients. I might say to a client, 'OK let's do some brainstorming for a minute about the possible reasons why this relationship might not be working'. The importance of brainstorming is that you don't evaluate as you go along, so you can come out with the most far-fetched of possible reasons, to be evaluated later. In the course of a brainstorming session, I might raise the concept of a hidden agenda, and later look at the possibility more closely, talk about it and see whether or not it may be operating for this client at this time. But I am against the notion that, because you are a counsellor, you almost need to have X-ray vision and be able to see hidden agendas on the basis of very minimal data. You may have a hunch, but you may have to wait and test it out.

Antonio Branco Vasco: I would like to ask you a question about the counsellor's tasks. Would you agree with Michael Mahoney (1986) that there is such a thing as a 'tyranny of technique', and that what is important is the message you transmit to clients rather than the technique itself?

Windy Dryden: Well, that may be true under certain conditions, but don't forget that clients often get messages they wouldn't receive otherwise, as a result of techniques. For example, let's take the task of exposing yourself to a feared object. Research is reasonably robust on this issue and shows that, if you really want to overcome your fears of particular objects, animals or specific situations, it is important to expose yourself to them. Now, what happens is that after you have exposed yourself to them, you get the 'message' that the horrible thing you thought would happen hasn't happened, e.g. the snake you thought was going to bite you or kill you is really manageable. Now you wouldn't have got that message if you hadn't learnt the techniques.

So I would readily agree with Mahoney if by 'tyranny of technique' he means that too much emphasis is placed on technique to the detriment of other aspects of the alliance. But I also think that clients won't get these helpful therapeutic self-messages if they don't learn some of these techniques. So I would partly agree with him and partly take issue with him.

Antonio Branco Vasco: The problem is that the technique is ineffective if the client doesn't get the message, so the crucial point is the impact of the message on the client.

Windy Dryden: Yes, that's right, but then it is hard to think of an effective technique that would not alter the client's messages. Techniques can't be looked at in isolation, and any behavioural technique has cognitive implications. You cannot separate out cognition and emotion from behaviour, so any of these domains are bound to be affected by technique.

Antonio Branco Vasco: Is there a danger though that counsellors may favour a restricted range of techniques?

Windy Dryden: Quite so. Arnold Lazarus has argued that, if you only have one technique, which is equivalent to a hammer, all you can do is bang nails in and smash things up, whereas a variety of techniques corresponds to a variety of tools. But having techniques at your disposal doesn't mean that you are able to use them with subtlety and discrimination. So I would say that skill is required in each of the three domains of the alliance.

Skilled counsellors of whatever persuasion need to master the technical aspects of their craft, but they also need to be able to relate to a variety of people and to keep in mind the direction of the endeavour, so that the relationship or the technical skill doesn't become an end in itself. Counsellors also need to have a humble view of their talents in all three domains and realise that no matter how skilful, both technically and interpersonally, and how mindful of the goals they are, they might not be the right person for a particular client. So I would like to emphasise the interdependence of the three aspects of the alliance, as well as the importance of taking a fairly realistic view of yourself as a counsellor, so that you would keep updating your talents while being aware of your limitations. This applies to counsellors of all persuasions not just to RET practitioners.

Chapter 4
Eclecticism and Integration

Antonio Branco Vasco: Integration and eclecticism in counselling and psychotherapy are fashionable topics. What are your views on these issues?

Windy Dryden: Well, eclecticism and integration have been defined in many different ways over the recent years. Whereas from the mid-1970s to the early 1980s 'eclecticism' was perhaps the preferred term, now there seems to be a definite preference for the term 'integration'. For example, there is a Society for the Exploration of Psychotherapy Integration (SEPI) as well as a new *Journal of Psychotherapy Integration* which supersedes the *Journal of Integrative and Eclectic Psychotherapy* as the main journal in the field. Note that the word 'eclectic' has been dropped from the new journal.

I actually prefer the word 'eclectic' to the word 'integrationist' or 'integrative'. Eclecticism means choosing what appears to the clinician to be the best from diverse systems, styles and schools, without trying to integrate them into a whole, whereas integration does entail bringing different elements into a whole. I would agree with Arnold Lazarus (1990) that we are not in a position to do this, since we don't have an agreed over-arching theory that would enable us to carry out this project. I think we are actually quite a long way from integration in that sense.

A number of people have put forward various theoretical models which, as far as I can see, are bids to be a way of integrating what I think is still a rather disparate field. These models are acceptable at the level of exploration – we must realise that this field is still in a very early phase of development. The problem is that people are integrating too quickly, without a strong foundation. Therefore, I prefer to use the term 'theoretically consistent eclecticism' which involves having a broad theoretical framework that serves to guide our choice of a wide variety of techniques. Arnold Lazarus argues that this term is virtually synonymous with technical eclecticism.

There are various strands to my own particular brand of theoretically consistent eclecticism, or technical eclecticism. Rational–emotive theory is the main cornerstone for understanding disturbance, but I also use the concept of the therapeutic alliance, as we have already discussed, as a way of bringing to bear far more general principles on the formation and development of therapeutic relationships.

Another strand is the notion of 'challenging but not overwhelming', which means that the counsellor needs to moderate the degree of disequilibrium experienced by the client at any one time. I think that change comes from the right amount of disequilibrium, so that if a therapeutic relationship is too smooth it will not stimulate change, whilst if it is too overwhelming, it is likely to frighten the client and therefore also prevent change. Challenge needs to be based on a responsible and effective therapeutic alliance.

These are the three main principles that inform my own eclectic approach (Dryden, 1987). I borrow quite widely in terms of technical procedures from a whole host of different schools, without in any way upholding the original theoretical rationale for the development of a particular technique. That's very much where I stand at the moment on the issue of integration and eclecticism.

Antonio Branco Vasco: So, you think that it is important to have a coherent theoretical framework, even though you feel free to use techniques from other schools.

Windy Dryden: That's right. I don't see how you can approach counselling without some kind of theoretical perspective. I think it was Cornsweet (1983) who actually stated that and certain philosophers of science have indicated that observations are not neutral but based on theoretical predispositions. My personal criterion in assessing a theory is coherence. Various other people, such as Kurt Lewin and Hans Eysenck, have argued that there is 'nothing so practical as a good theory'.

Antonio Branco Vasco: Is rational–emotive theory good in this sense?

Windy Dryden: I think it's reasonably good as a theoretical system, in that it describes a number of different levels of cognitive change.

First of all there is the evaluative level, which refers to the fact that humans bring to situations a tendency to evaluate; secondly, there is the inferential level, which means that humans have a tendency to interpret what they see.

Rational–emotive theory can also account for behavioural change in which the evaluative and inferential levels are perhaps not so involved, as well as for situation changes. So it is a pretty powerful attempt to account for different levels of change.

Unfortunately, the research literature on rational–emotive theory isn't that good, because most of the studies haven't really tested its basic tenets, such as the role of rational and irrational evaluations. Until recently, most of the scales which purported to measure rational and irrational beliefs did not have good face validity nor did they keenly discriminate between rational and irrational beliefs. At present, work going on at the Institute for RET in New York is attempting to put that straight. So I think that the rational–emotive account of psychological disturbance and of change needs to be tested empirically in a more formal fashion, although I find it helpful as a way of making sense of the clinical information that is before me.

Another important concept for me is Arnold Lazarus's (1989) idea that we are not just cognitive, emotive and behavioural individuals, we also have other modalities. I use a number of such concepts in my overall model of clinical decision-making.

I think that the role of a framework is to help you to make decisions. If there is one truism about clinical work, it is that you are constantly having to make decisions, although you need to take into account the input of the client's decisions too, as we discussed earlier. It is the interaction between the counsellor, as a decision-maker, and the client, as a decision-maker, that is very important.

Anyway, I do think it is important to have a broad theoretical perspective on counselling, although I couldn't say that all the ideas I use from the growing literature really fit together in one neat coherent package. At the moment I am happy to use rational–emotive theory as my main theoretical resource, but there may well be a time when I have a theoretical revolution on my hands, as Thomas Kuhn would say, and adopt another more encompassing theory. But I find RET theory to be the most pragmatic at the moment.

Antonio Branco Vasco: So you believe that RET has a strong heuristic value for clinical decision-making, whether or not it is successful in explaining human behaviour and change.

Windy Dryden: I do think it has the potential to account for emotional disturbance and change. The problem is that the studies which have been done have not properly tested hypotheses derived from rational–emotive theory. Most of the studies which have been done on rational–emotive therapy as a clinical method, for example, have not shown clearly that what they were investigating was a competent example of RET.

So there is a sense in which my allegiance to rational–emotive theory is a bit of a leap of faith. I think that we need to take a sceptical look at the available evidence and at the ways that some of the concepts have been operationalised. So when I say that I am happy to use rational–emotive theory as a major theoretical framework, it is always with a sense of unease, because I am quite aware that its empirical foundations really need to be much firmer than they are at the moment.

Antonio Branco Vasco: It has been argued that RET is a loose set of principles with no conceptual coherence. What are your views on this criticism?

Windy Dryden: Well, I don't think Ellis has ever put forward a *formal* theory of personality and personality change, although there have been attempts to do that in other approaches; for example, Carl Rogers did that for client-centred therapy in 1959 and RET would perhaps benefit from a similar formal statement. But it is interesting that we started off with a consideration of eclecticism and integration and are now moving back to RET. It is probably because I have written about rational–emotive therapy as one of the main foundations of my eclectic approach to psychotherapy. Ellis (1987) has actually written an article in which he argued that rational–emotive therapy was one of the first integrative approaches to counselling and psychotherapy, in that it has integrated cognition, affect and behaviour ever since 1962. But I don't think that RET alone, without the added ingredients I mentioned earlier, is sufficient as a broad eclectic approach to counselling. So perhaps we should move back to eclecticism and integration.

Antonio Branco Vasco: Would you agree that there is an overlap between the question of eclecticism and integration, on the one hand, and the question of common factors and specific factors in counselling, on the other?

Windy Dryden: Yes. In my review of Garfield's chapter in Norcross's (1986) *Handbook of Eclectic Psychotherapy*, I argued that whilst Garfield had done a really good job of articulating common factors, what he had failed to do sufficiently, to my taste anyway, was to help the clinician to make decisions. It's one thing to know that there are various common factors in counselling, but it is another to know what to do with this knowledge.

How does knowledge of common factors alone help the clinician to make decisions from moment to moment? I mean, how *do* you know when to utilise reinforcement as opposed to suggestion? I found that this was lacking in Garfield's account in Norcross's book.

Now, you have recently edited a book on common factors, so perhaps I could ask *you* a question, at this stage. How do you think knowledge of common therapeutic factors can help counsellors to make moment-by-moment decisions at the technical and strategic levels?

Antonio Branco Vasco: I would definitely agree with you. It is important to be aware of the basic similarity of what people do in counselling, irrespective of orientation, but I think that such knowledge will not provide you with a guide to clinical decision-making. That's the most crucial point.

Windy Dryden: Right. So you agree with me. But having criticised Garfield's work, let me say that I think he has, together with Jerome Frank, made a really good contribution by showing the reality of a common ground among orientations, and thus has helped to initiate the debate that both we and SEPI members are engaged in. A political analogy could be Jimmy Carter's role in providing a forum for Israel and Egypt to come together at Camp David. Garfield's major contribution has been to provide a way of bringing people from disparate systems together, and thus advancing a debate that may have been quite difficult otherwise.

Antonio Branco Vasco: The concept of 'marker' is also a step forward towards integration in counselling, and is very important for clinical decision-making. What are your views on this?

Windy Dryden: First of all what do you mean by the term 'marker'?

Antonio Branco Vasco: I mean the identification of some sign in the client, showing that an intervention is needed at that moment.

Windy Dryden: I think there are two sets of markers that we as counsellors need to be aware of. First of all there are markers that we perceive in the client – and those markers that we observe will be largely determined by our theoretical position: the wider our theoretical perspective, presumably the more markers we would be able to identify.

There are also markers within the counsellor's experience, and I think that in this particular respect rational–emotive therapy is lacking, which is partly why I have looked elsewhere for therapeutic guidance. RET is not one of the therapies that encourage the practitioner to look within him- or herself that much. Markers within ourselves are important, not only to understand the client, but also perhaps to become aware of how we as counsellors may be interfering, sometimes terminally so, in the counselling process. No doubt, somebody in the not too distant future will come up with an approach to integrative or eclectic counselling and psychotherapy which will be largely based on a taxonomy of markers.

Antonio Branco Vasco: Do you think that people within the field of eclecticism and integration draw sufficiently on one another's work?

Windy Dryden: One of the main concerns that I articulated in my chapter in Norcross's book (Dryden, 1986) was just that – the extent to which eclectic and integrative theorists make use of each other's work, and I am still concerned about this. It is possible for me to extend the range of concepts that I make use of. For example, I find Prochaska and DiClemente's (1986) concepts of stages of change – in their transtheoretical approach to eclecticism – very helpful, because when we are trying to make sense of rifts in the therapeutic relationship, a good question to ask ourselves is, 'Am I assuming that the client is in a more (or less) advanced stage of change than he or she actually is in?'. That's a good concept to use.

Antonio Branco Vasco: Do you have any examples from your practice to illustrate the importance of the 'stages of change' concept?

Windy Dryden: Yes, there are a number of cases that come to mind, mainly from my experience as a supervisor. One of the issues that I often point out to my RET supervisees concerns their assumption that their client is ready to change when that is not necessarily the case. When clients have ambivalent feelings about changing, you really need to spend time in the early stages of the therapeutic sequence. But such practitioners are often quite keen to start challenging irrational beliefs, and consequently they can bring about rifts in the therapeutic alliance by assuming that the client is in, say, the contemplation stage of change or even the action stage of change, whereas the client is in reality in the pre-contemplation stage. This is a phenomenon that I come across quite frequently when I supervise rational–emotive therapists.

Antonio Branco Vasco: Is that another way of looking at what you call in RET 'too much too soon'?

Windy Dryden: That's right. I remember that when Paul Wachtel tried to integrate analytical and behavioural therapies, he was accused by his psychoanalytical colleagues of having excessive therapeutic zeal. And I think that some RET therapists can definitely be accused of having excessive therapeutic zeal.

Antonio Branco Vasco: What do you think are the limits of integration and eclecticism?

Windy Dryden: Whereas many helpful concepts are emerging in the field that is now called psychotherapy integration, I still think it has its limitations. First, there have been various cautionary comments, mainly voiced by Stanley Messer (1990) who has argued that different approaches, and the techniques that they have spawned, are based on different epistemologies and visions of reality and, secondly, all eclectics and integrationists are partisan to some degree and emphasise certain principles and de-emphasise others. Take somebody like Arnold Lazarus who is broad in his view of human behaviour in terms of the seven modalities of the BASIC ID and broad in his utilisation of techniques (Lazarus, 1989). His approach is based on social learning theory; now if we ask what he doesn't include in his system, this is almost as revealing as what he does include. So

I think that what is happening is that we are almost entering a 'paradigmatic' phase of eclecticism and integration, in which many people are developing their own different brands and emphases – based on partisan ideas. The danger is that many different schools of integration may develop. Joseph Hart (1986) has stated that this diversity is all to the good, and that he wouldn't be concerned if there were as many brands of integrative and eclectic therapy as there are practitioners. I personally think this is taking things a bit too far!

Antonio Branco Vasco: Do you think that the integrative movement is encouraging counsellors to be less dogmatic and more mindful of research results?

Windy Dryden: Well, I think that one of the important by-products of the eclectic and integrative movement is that counsellors are reading more and more widely, rather than limiting themselves to the literature of their own particular orientation – as used to be the case for all brands of therapy, from psychoanalysis to behaviour therapy. That would be a significant achievement for the integrative movement.

Whether practitioners will also utilise research findings more it's too early to say. Of course they all say they will, but actually to do so is another matter entirely, and this raises a very interesting research question. But even if the movement only achieves the former of these goals, I think it will have been quite helpful.

Another question which arises, in relation to research, is whether we have robust enough evidence that eclectic and integrative approaches are more effective than non-eclectic ones. I think we need to prove that this movement is more than a way of bringing practitioners together. This would be important in itself, but it wouldn't be sufficient if it didn't filter through to the people who matter, i.e. the clients. We need to investigate whether the client is better served by going to see an eclectic or a non-eclectic therapist. Indeed, there is tentative evidence against the greater effectiveness of eclectic and integrative therapy. Some research shows that adherence to 'manualised' therapy seems to be related to client outcome to some degree, so that practitioners who stick to the principles of one school may be bringing about a better outcome than those who belong to the same school but are less 'pure'. All this makes for a really interesting decade ahead in research.

Antonio Branco Vasco: So, to sum up, where do you think the integrative movement will lead us in the next 20 or 30 years?

Windy Dryden: It's difficult to say, but I fear that people in academic and clinical careers might feel that they have to keep producing yet new emphases and new brands of eclectic and integrative psychotherapy, which would stress difference at the expense of similarity. I think that would be a great shame, although I can understand why it would occur, because academic promotion tends to come from presenting our own theories and approaches as unique and perhaps better than competing theories and approaches.

I also think that the future of this area is related to the destiny of psychology as a whole. Arthur Staats (1983) has argued that psychology is in a crisis of disunity and that there is a need to come up with a unified science. This is very similar to what some people in the integrative movement have been saying.

Another trend that is already beginning to become apparent is an increased emphasis on interdisciplinary work. As discipline barriers break down, counsellors and psychotherapists will be able to learn from and contribute to the work of sociologists, biologists, anthropologists, economists and so on. On the one hand, I would like to see more of that but, on the other, I find it a daunting prospect, because it's hard enough for me to find the time to keep up with research findings, theoretical developments, practical innovations both in rational–emotive therapy and in integration and eclecticism. Who would have the time to keep up with other areas as well? Anyway, I think it needs to be done and probably will be. One of the things I would like SEPI to do in the next decade is to have one or two conferences on interdisciplinary work as it impinges on psychotherapy integration. I am sure that this will occur.

One caution here: when, and if, we move towards this interdisciplinary work, which I predict is going to happen, I do hope that whoever is in the vanguard will be able to write very simply and for practitioners. Some of the major writers in fields such as evolution, biology and the philosophy of science write at such a high level that their ideas will not easily filter down to practitioners. Please write simply for simple folk like myself!

Antonio Branco Vasco: Do you think that non-scientific forms of healing – what is usually called traditional healing – also have something to teach counsellors?

Windy Dryden: Well, traditional forms of healing are only non-scientific because we have a tough time bringing the scientific tradition to bear on them, but some of the work done on witch-doctors, for example, could easily be put within the scientific tradition, and in fact I think it has been done. Yes, I think we have a lot to learn from that. We also need to understand more about how cults work, develop and break down. What we are really talking about here is understanding human change from a variety of different perspectives.

Chapter 5
For Clients

Antonio Branco Vasco: What would be your advice to people who feel in need of psychological help?

Windy Dryden: The stage when people become aware of having emotional or behavioural problems could be referred to as the interface between what Prochaska and DiClemente (1986) have called the pre-contemplation and the contemplation stages of change. People in Britain have a number of options: they could talk about it with friends, but with increasing frequency they are turning to agony aunts and uncles in magazines and on the radio, getting advice of varying quality.

The number of articles about counselling and psychotherapy in the British press also seems to be increasing. Indeed, counselling is enjoying quite a good press in Britain at the moment. There is even a late night counselling programme on television, which apparently has a very good audience. So the more it becomes acceptable to read and talk about these things, the more people will consider consulting counsellors and psychotherapists.

I think that people can derive quite a lot of benefit from talking to friends, relatives, priests, rabbis and so on, and I certainly don't believe that psychological change is the sole province of counsellors and psychotherapists. But if a potential client has unsuccessfully tried these routes, or actually prefers to consult a professional, it is very difficult at the moment to know precisely how to go about it. A very small minority of clients go to academic libraries and do their own research. I have heard of cases of clients who actually looked at the research literature, realised that the best approach for their specific phobia was some kind of behaviour therapy, and actively sought out behaviour therapists. But that is quite rare.

Earlier I mentioned the idea of a therapeutic matchmaker. That was half serious and half fanciful, but I would like to see some kind of national network in Britain, coordinated by independent people who were quite knowledgeable about what was available in different parts of the country, so that they would be able to gather and put together relevant information from clients and from counsellors. That's a dream of mine and one of these days I might get round to doing something about it. In the interim, what I would advise people to do is to get some evidence that whoever they are consulting has a recognised qualification.

Antonio Branco Vasco: Should training courses be accredited as well as individuals?

Windy Dryden: At the moment the British Association for Counselling is in the business of beginning to evaluate and recognise different training courses, as they do in the States. Clinical psychologists all come from courses that are fairly regularly visited by a panel of experts from the British Psychological Society to ensure that standards are being maintained. Also there is now a United Kingdom Standing Conference of Psychotherapy (UKSCP) that is moving towards the registration of psychotherapists, mainly through membership of member organisations. That's somewhat problematic for me personally, because the Institute of Rational–Emotive Therapy in Britain has only three trained members at the moment and there has to be a minimum of 50 members in order to become a fully paid-up organisational member of the UKSCP! So ironically I may not be on their register, although I am going to fight that when the time comes! Thus, there will be three major ways of satisfying yourself that the person you are consulting has at least been properly trained.

Antonio Branco Vasco: Can you outline one of the approaches currently used in Britain to accredit practitioners?

Windy Dryden: The British Association for Counselling has a very interesting and helpful system of accreditation for individual practitioners. It stipulates certain criteria that you have to meet in order to become an accredited practitioner, but their accreditation only lasts for 5 years, after which you have to re-apply showing that you have had continuing supervision and have pursued professional development activities. Their criteria are really quite stringent, and quite a few people in the States would not be accredited if BAC guidelines were applied there. People who have been licensed there seem to have a rather lax attitude towards continuing supervision. I am always having a go at my fellow rational–emotive therapists, either Associate Fellows or Fellows of the Institute for RET, because they don't get regular supervision.

I have had ongoing peer supervision with Dr Ruth Wessler, a noted RET supervisor in the States for over 10 years, and once I worked out that she and I are the most frequently supervised RET therapists in the world!

Antonio Branco Vasco: Based on what you have just said, how would you advise potential clients?

Windy Dryden: My advice to potential clients would be to consult somebody who has some standing in the professional community. I think it is best to avoid answering advertisements in newspapers, unless you can satisfy yourself that the person who is advertising his or her services is a member of a respected· professional organisation – such as the ones I mentioned earlier. Having said that, the fact that a counsellor has a good professional reputation doesn't mean that he or she will be right for you. I realise that it may be difficult for people in great personal distress to shop around for the right counsellor in the private sector, but that is actually what I do recommend.

Antonio Branco Vasco: If a client is prepared to shop around, what advice would you give him or her?

Windy Dryden: When you consult counsellors, you could begin by saying that you would like to talk to them about the possibility of becoming a client and to find out a bit more about their work and whether their approach is going to match your needs. As you do this, pay attention to how they treat you. Are they welcoming? Are they professional? Are they respectful? Do they listen? Can you imagine really confiding your problems to them? Are they willing to talk to you openly about their therapeutic approach? I realise that this last piece of advice may be biased against some psychoanalytical practitioners, because this would be against their normal practice.

Another piece of advice would be: as you ask for this

information, does the counsellor treat it as a legitimate request or does he or she tend to pathologise it? Does he or she regard it as part of your problem? If he or she does, my advice is not to consult him or her.

Now, this is complicated by the fact that clients may well settle for a counsellor who makes them feel too comfortable. And I really think, as I have said before, that it is important to manage the tension between comfortable equilibrium and overwhelming disequilibrium, to reach a situation that is challenging but not overwhelming. In this case my advice to clients would be to realise that counselling and psychotherapy may well involve disequilibrium, and to be sceptical if the counsellor they are consulting seems to give them too comfortable a ride. But all this is quite a hell of a burden to place on prospective clients, so perhaps the main piece of advice is simply to notice whether the person is respectful, whether he or she treats your questions as legitimate, and whether he or she seems generally concerned about you within a professional context. Be very sceptical if you get any sense of under-involvement or over-involvement and give such counsellors a wide berth.

Antonio Branco Vasco: Apart from what you have just said, do you think that a rational decision in choosing a counsellor should be based mainly on compatibility and matching world views, or on the kind of problems you have as a client?

Windy Dryden: Well, both, although I think they do overlap to some degree. One of the ways clients can do this is by consulting one of the various textbooks being published in Britain which provide an introduction to different approaches to counselling and psychotherapy written in lay terms.

I mentioned earlier that I am often struck when I hear that clients have actually looked at my book *Individual Therapy in Britain* (Dryden, 1984c), read about different approaches and, having found one they resonated with, got in touch with the relevant contact address given in the book and sought out a counsellor from the orientation of their choice.

A 'consumers' guide' for the British market needs to include unbiased information on the kind of problems that an approach is particularly suited for, the assumptions it makes about human nature and change, and so on.

Having said that, this does make life hard for the growing number of integrative and eclectic counsellors, because it is more difficult to communicate clearly about these approaches within a 'consumers' guide' context. However, a number of clients are beginning to become aware of this trend and, as a result, are looking for counsellors who take an integrative or eclectic approach.

Antonio Branco Vasco: I would say that potential clients also need to consult practitioners who are themselves free from psychological disturbance. To this end do you think that trainee counsellors should be required to undergo personal therapy?

Windy Dryden: That's a very interesting point. Generally I am ambivalent about it, although I am aware that the requirement of personal therapy is part of a trend towards ensuring that practitioners are professionally prepared and satisfy the standards of the organisation that gives them a stamp of approval. I am ambivalent about the issue because I don't think that personal therapy should be imposed on people. However, I believe that if you are going to enter the field, you should have *some* experience of being a client yourself in order to understand your clients' experiences better. As a result, I have been ambivalent about making personal therapy a requirement for the trainees on the MSc in Counselling course that I direct at Goldsmiths' College. I recently made a decision to introduce this as a requirement because I don't want my students to be unfavourably dealt with in the future, when it might become difficult to be accredited without it. Nevertheless, I am by no means thoroughly comfortable with the idea because I am against counselling being imposed on people.

Antonio Branco Vasco: How do you deal with clients who come to see you but refuse to recognise they have a problem and only blame other people, partners, friends and so on?

Windy Dryden: Well, I deal with it by acknowledging to myself that the person is in a pre-contemplative stage of change and is also likely to be in a lot of psychological pain; therefore I attempt to respond quite empathically to both these situations. I would hear that as a signal that they are in a distressing situation and as a request to make their relationships better. If they come on their own, I would invite them to bring their partner, or whoever it is, with them.

It is easy to frighten clients away by confronting them too quickly and categorically refusing to have anything to do with other people in their lives; therefore it is a good idea to bear in mind the 'challenging but not overwhelming' principle mentioned earlier and to try and keep the challenge low, yet without going along with their view that others are to blame for their plight.

Once I was 'ordered' by a man to go round and see his wife and command her to be a good wife! My response then was to show my understanding of his pain and to suggest that I see both him and his wife, but the guy was adamant in his request. That kind of situation is difficult for any counsellor to deal with, particularly if the client has a fixed idea and won't respond to the counsellor's empathy as a way of creating a forum to talk about the problem.

Antonio Branco Vasco: Would you advocate compulsory counselling or therapy for criminals?

Windy Dryden: Well, no, not if you put it like that! It sounds a bit like the tyranny of psychotherapy. I could imagine that somebody like Jeffrey Masson (1988) would be quick to come down on an endeavour like that. I personally don't work with criminals, but I know that clinical psychologists are active in British prisons today. Again, it's a question of how to encourage people to move from a pre-contemplative to a contemplative stage of change: you cannot *make* somebody move from one stage to another, but you can help them with ways of reflecting on their crimes as a means of moving them forwards.

What may be particularly helpful in this context is the use of people who have been in similar situations and have successfully made use of psychotherapeutic services. That is why a number of addiction services use recovering addicts to show that change is possible. Former addicts are the living proof of that possibility, and probably also know a lot about the manoeuvres that people may utilise to stay in the pre-contemplative stage of change.

I could imagine that happening in prisons, but I would be against it being carried out against people's will. I think there are ways of getting people interested in psychotherapeutic services without turning these into a tyranny. Once they become a tyranny they cease to deserve the term 'therapeutic'.

Antonio Branco Vasco: Some people reject the idea of going into counselling because they see it as a sign of weakness and think that, if they were stronger, they would be able to bear their suffering on their own, without a counsellor's help. What would you say to such a person?

Windy Dryden: Well, there are a number of things that can be said. First of all, I empathise with that position – it is something that is often expressed at the beginning of counselling – but I also say that seeking help can be seen as a sign of strength! There is a phrase I often quote under these circumstances: 'Only you can do it but you don't have to do it alone', which clearly indicates that although we are responsible for our own change, we can often utilise a bit of help along the way.

Another thing I often do is to ask my clients what they would do if their best friend came to them and asked for help with a particular problem, which is exactly the same problem as the client is talking about. Would they consider them weak? Would they say to them, 'Look, you are weak, you are shameful, get out of my house!'. Or would they have a more compassionate attitude towards their friend? If they say that they wouldn't view their friend as weak, I might point out that it's possible to take the same attitude towards themselves as they take towards their friend.

The development and maintenance of a therapeutic alliance with such people who John Bowlby called 'compulsively self-reliant' really has to encompass and respect their strong desire for autonomy; and I always try to indicate overtly and covertly that counselling will increase their autonomy rather than take it away from them.

Antonio Branco Vasco: That raises an interesting point about the therapeutic relationship being a relationship of authority. What would you say to clients who may feel they are not getting anywhere in counselling and yet are somehow afraid to discuss this with their counsellors?

Windy Dryden: Again, that is an interesting issue. There may be a need for an advisory service for clients at some point – or, as Dave Mearns has suggested, a self-help group for clients in which they can talk to each other about their therapy as it unfolds. I would encourage people to be honest with their counsellors, but also to try and look at their fears, see whether they are familiar and belong to a pattern, and to take the risk and confront these fears. If they feel unable to do this, and the counsellor hasn't brought the issue to their attention, it may be a sign that this particular therapeutic relationship isn't working, so perhaps they should consider going to another counsellor.

Another possibility for clients might be to express their concern in a letter to their counsellor – this might be discussed at the next session, or the counsellor might also reply in writing. Some counsellors might view these ideas askance, but what we are really talking about here is flexibility, novel ways of handling problems – concepts like the development of a therapeutic matchmaking service, self-help groups for clients and so on.

Antonio Branco Vasco: So what you are again emphasising here is therapeutic flexibility.

Windy Dryden: Although counsellors of course need to have their own views about disturbance, they should also be sufficiently flexible and sensitive to their clients' needs, rather than shove them all into one mould. There is a lovely phrase which was originally used about Arnold Lazarus's therapeutic approach but is now used more broadly, and that is the concept of 'bespoke therapy'. If you needed a suit in the old days you wouldn't have one off the peg, but you would go and see a tailor who would take precise measurements down to a quarter of an inch and really take the trouble to fit the suit to your requirements, even if it meant taking it back two or three times.

This metaphor can be applied to the therapeutic relationship, albeit with a difference: the counsellor should be flexible, but not give the clients exactly what they want, because quite frequently what clients want is to rid themselves of their symptoms without changing – I am not advocating that. If I could give one piece of advice to a client, it would be to choose a flexible therapist or counsellor.

Antonio Branco Vasco: Does that also mean that counsellors should frequently ask their clients if they feel comfortable with what is happening in the sessions?

Windy Dryden: I wouldn't use the word comfortable here. I am suggesting that counselling should be helpful rather than comfortable – and what is helpful is not always comfortable. But you are right in that the counsellor should be flexible enough to ask that question, and to listen sceptically but respectfully to the answer. If I were to sum up my advice to counsellors it would be to be flexible.

Antonio Branco Vasco: Any final advice for clients?

Windy Dryden: I would address them in these words: 'Don't expect that all your problems will disappear as a result of going for counselling. If it is successful you will be able to get "unstuck" and move on, but I would like to see you moving on with particular coping skills that you can call upon whenever you encounter problematic situations in the future'. An important study (Maluccio, 1979) showed that clients benefited from therapeutic services in that they were helped to utilise their environment more creatively, to go out and get help and support from friends, relatives or other agencies. There is something really very dangerous in the notion that the counsellor is somehow the sole therapeutic agent in a person's life. That's a different kind of tyranny – it's the omnipotence of the counsellor and I really think we have to guard against that in this field. We can be very important in a client's life, but hopefully we don't replace their important interpersonal relationships; we can help them to benefit more from these and perhaps to become more 'therapeutic' for others as well.

Chapter 6
Client Deterioration and Counsellor Burn-out

Antonio Branco Vasco: Is counselling always beneficial, or can it have iatrogenic effects?

Windy Dryden: I will answer this question on the basis both of my own experience – of supervising other therapists and talking to clients – and of the growing research literature on the subject. I'm very much in accord with a study done by Grunebaum (1986) on harmful psychotherapeutic experiences. He found that the two main ways in which you could have negative effects in psychotherapy were through a counsellor's under-involvement or over-involvement in the process.

Let me consider under-involvement first. Here, such counsellors are perceived as cold and withdrawn, and seem to make little or no attempt to show basic human qualities. Incidentally, I have never actually understood how coldness, withdrawnness and neutrality could have any positive therapeutic effect, because if that were the case people who had cold, withdrawn, uninvolved parents would presumably not be 'harmed' by it. Anyway, I think that when the counsellor either puts on a mask of detachment or is, in fact, detached, there can be harmful consequences. This might apply to some of the less skilful psychoanalytical therapists, who seem to take the concept of neutrality far too literally. I think you can be fairly neutral in the process of counselling without being cold, aloof and withholding. It is not the neutrality of counsellors that is potentially harmful, but the failure to demonstrate decent human qualities, because these are needed in counselling perhaps more than in any other field. In my case, however, the aloofness of my third therapist whom I discussed in Chapter 1 had a helpful impact, since my decision to help myself through means other than psychotherapy was partly in response to his coldness. So I am not saying that being exposed to a cold, aloof therapist *always* has harmful effects – as you know I am against statements that involve 'always' and 'never', but I think there is a general pattern, as Grunebaum seemed to find.

The second pattern is the counsellor's over-involvement which can lead to serious infringement of boundaries. The therapists in Grunebaum's study seemed to initiate their clients into a kind of therapeutic 'cult'! I think that harmful experiences definitely occur when counsellors have sex with their clients, although theoretically some people would probably say that having had sex with their counsellor has helped them in some way.

Other forms of over-involvement include becoming friends with clients or using them in other ways, such as getting them to do jobs for you in return for payment. I think that this muddies the waters. One of the reasons I am against the general principle of counsellors becoming friends with their clients is that friendship is much more reciprocal in nature. I am not saying that counselling is totally one way, but essentially you are there for the client, and I think that some counsellors who get over-involved are mainly there for themselves, even though they pretend otherwise.

Recently, for example, I read in a local newspaper that a hypnotherapist had been taken to court for having at least one, and possibly more, sexual experiences with female clients. He claimed that it was part of the treatment! Whether he was so deluded that he really believed it or used it as a defence I don't know, but that kind of over-involvement is definitely negative and iatrogenic.

Another negative factor would be where a counsellor gets very angry with his or her clients. This can stem from the demand that the client shouldn't be as difficult as he or she is, or that they should be making more progress. Counsellors can interpret lack of progress as a threat to their self-esteem, and if they demand that they *must* be good counsellors they could also demand that their clients must validate that view of themselves. I think that if a counsellor's anger is overtly displayed in an attacking manner it can be quite an iatrogenic factor. So these are the three main factors that immediately come to mind.

Antonio Branco Vasco: The literature also shows that intimate relationships between counsellors and former clients rarely work very well.

Windy Dryden: Yes. I think that this phenomenon happens much more frequently than we would have anticipated. I am not sure quite how well they do work out – I will take your word for it that they don't – but that wouldn't surprise me.

Antonio Branco Vasco: So do you think it would be wise for clients to resist getting involved in such situations?

Windy Dryden: Yes. Clients should be highly sceptical of counsellors who seem to want to involve them in activities that common-sense tells them would be unprofessional. However, it may be very difficult for clients to know what constitutes unprofessional counsellor behaviour. Where do you draw the line between positive therapeutic factors such as interest, warmth and empathy, and unethical over-involvement? Some of my person-centred colleagues talk about the insufficiency of an hour a week of these core conditions, so some of them have experimented with extending the therapeutic hour, going for walks with their clients and so on. I think you have to be really very careful in these situations, and discuss your motives in supervision, because you could easily masquerade your need for gratification as innovations to help the client. You have to watch that.

Antonio Branco Vasco: How do you think all this relates to the phenomenon of 'drop-outs' in counselling?

Windy Dryden: Well, it's certainly easier to drop out from an under-involved counsellor than from an over-involved one. It may be very difficult to get out of an over-involved relationship, particularly if that has been a pattern that the client has experienced before. Here I want to put most of the onus on the counsellor, because I think it's the counsellor's job to maintain a healthy boundary, but it wouldn't surprise me if the clients who become over-involved in therapeutic relationships were over-involved in other relationships too. The reason why it can be hard to break out of these relationships is that clients may well get something out of them. It's difficult to step back and be wary if the counsellor seems to be treating you as a 'special person', showing you a lot of warmth, and wants to extend the relationship.

It is easier to get out of under-involved relationships, where the person doesn't feel understood or listened to, doesn't feel that he or she is being considered as a person, and so on.

It is also hard to get out of a therapeutic relationship when the counsellor interprets your wish to leave as a sign of your problem. My particular stance on this issue is that it needs to be looked at, but I would certainly not interpret the client's desire to leave counselling as a 'sickness' – as part of his or her problem. In general, then, I think that once counselling gets stuck in an over-involved or under-involved type of groove, then we should be thankful if clients drop out before they are harmed.

Antonio Branco Vasco: We are moving to the topic of failures in counselling and psychotherapy. What do you think the most important causes of failures are?

Windy Dryden: I think we have to be quite clear about what we mean by failure. Failure from whose perspective? I'd like to deal with this issue by presuming that failure in counselling and psychotherapy occurs either when clients improve only marginally, making slight changes but nothing that will really enhance the quality of their life, or when they don't make any progress at all, and even get worse.

I think that this failure can be looked at in terms of client factors, counsellor factors or the interaction between the two. Again I find it helpful to use Bordin's (1979) concept of the therapeutic alliance as a way of making sense of this issue.

Let me look at the *bond* domain first. When failure can be attributed to bond factors, clients tend not to feel understood and are not really engaged in counselling. They are not necessarily dealing with somebody who is cold and under-involved – as I was describing earlier – but there is a sense that the counsellor is mouthing the right words without really developing a relationship with the client.

Another important factor is when the counsellor doesn't vary his or her interpersonal style. Not all clients respond to empathy, warmth and genuineness: with some you need to be firm, whereas with others you can help best by being somewhat aloof, but without being disengaged.

An unwitting reinforcement of the client's own self-defeating interpersonal style, as when a very passive client elicits an over-active interpersonal response from the counsellor, is in my experience another potential cause of failure.

A major cause of failure in the *goal* domain of the alliance is when goals are not agreed upon or updated, and therefore there is a sense that the client wants to go in one direction and the counsellor in another.

In the *task* domain, failure can occur if the counsellor does not take into account whether or not the client can actually make use of the tasks of the therapy – for example a rational–emotive therapist expecting some clients to engage in the process of Socratic dialogue when they are not able to do this.

These are all speculations, albeit informed by my clinical and supervisory experience, and I am going to conduct a consumer-based study exploring the utility of the therapeutic alliance concept in understanding therapeutic failure. My view is that we can account for most instances of failure in terms of one or more aspects of the alliance.

Another important reason for failure is counsellor ignorance, and that is the reason why I think it is so important for practitioners to read the literature. For example, there is evidence now that treating panic disorders involves an explanation of the panic process, breathing retraining and an understanding of the role played by what Clark (1986) has called 'catastrophic interpretations'. If you follow these guide-lines, treatment of panic attacks can be a fairly short affair, whereas before it used to be notoriously difficult. But if you don't keep up with the literature as broadly as you can, and realise that there may be treatments of choice, such as exposure with phobic clients, response prevention with compulsive clients, and so on, then you are likely to fail, no matter how good you are at developing a therapeutic relationship.

Antonio Branco Vasco: Do you want to say something about your own failures as a counsellor?

Windy Dryden: Well, again my own failures as a counsellor can be explained in terms of the alliance. One example is when clients come in with a conceptualisation of their problems that is very much at variance with what I am offering them. Sometimes I get referrals for people who think that 'RET' stands for something other than what it is: a client may come in wanting Reichian therapy, for example, and when they hear my explanation of their problem they say 'well, let's forget it'. In the past I used to try and convince these people of my way of thinking, but now I have learnt to refer them on, although I might still share my perspective on things with them.

This is where I think there is a limit to how broad you can

be. I can't blend a cognitive system of explanation with a position that seems to locate psychological disturbance in energy blockages in the body.

So one way of reducing the number of failures would be to be selective in taking on clients, although there may be external pressures such as financial dependence on counselling as a livelihood, which operate against such selectivity. I also wonder how many failures could be avoided through more sensitive referral procedures. I certainly refer people whom I think would be better off seeing counsellors from other persuasions or female counsellors, for example. Funnily enough, I seem to get a number of calls from people who think that my name is 'Wendy' Dryden, or that Windy is a woman's name. I can hear their surprise and hesitation when I answer the phone and say that I am Windy Dryden, and I can almost predict that they want to see a woman. So I think that trying to meet clients' reasonable anticipations and preferences in therapy could actually obviate quite a few failures.

There are also a couple of client factors that I think are important. One factor is not taking responsibility for the change process, not doing homework assignments and so on. Here I am assuming that the client does understand the importance of this and yet still doesn't do it.

But then we come back to the old robust finding that probably the clients who fail the most are those who are more disturbed, and that's one of the problems that we need to address in counselling and psychotherapy – how to target our therapeutic services to those who really need them, whilst others may perhaps derive as much benefit from less intervention.

If we look at other relationship factors, it may occur that for one reason or another the counsellor and client just don't get on, are just not suited to each other. The idea that a counsellor may be able successfully to develop bonds with 99 per cent of clients seems to me again to conjure up the notion of conselor omnipotence.

In ordinary life people sometimes do take an instant dislike to one another; we could perhaps look at it in terms of transference or counter-transference, but the fact is that it happens, and I think that this could also account for failure. You may find yourself not looking forward to seeing particular clients, or hoping they will cancel, and clients may have similar feelings about you. Some therapeutic matches are not made in heaven! But if we talk about it with clients early enough in the process, then I think we can make sensible suggestions for them to consult other people who may be more suited to them.

Antonio Branco Vasco: Of course counselling may have detrimental effects on counsellors as well as on clients. Would you like to say something about the phenomenon of so-called burn-out?

Windy Dryden: My own particular approach to the burn-out problem is variety. I teach, I supervise, I see clients and I sometimes engage in social activities such as going on holiday – although not as frequently as my wife would like me to! Variety for me seems to be a way of protecting myself from burn-out.

I think we need to allow for the fact that people have different energy levels. I have a fairly high energy level and can do a fair amount, but other people don't, and I have heard some of my analytical colleagues complain of being very tired after seeing five clients in a day. So for them to take on six or seven would be problematic, whereas for me seeing six or seven clients a day wouldn't be too much of a problem. It is important to 'know thyself' in terms of energy level in order to know how much non-clinical time you need in your life and so on.

I think this touches on one of the real vulnerabilities for people in the helping professions and this is the ability to say no. If you get a referral for a new client and you haven't got a space, it may be tempting to fit them in at the end of the day, but I think it's important to be assertive and say no in order to protect yourself. If counsellors can't be good counsellors for themselves, it is doubtful whether they could be good models of mental health for their clients.

Antonio Branco Vasco: What do you think the main symptoms of burn-out are?

Windy Dryden: Some of the obvious ones include falling asleep or feeling very tired in sessions, general irritability, lapses of concentration, memory problems, boredom, interpersonal difficulties with your partner, and also I think a failure to be sensitive to your own bodily changes. This brings us back to the notion of the invulnerable, omnipotent counsellor – 'burn-out happens to other people, it doesn't happen to me!'

When I was at Aston University, for example, there were all kinds of interpersonal difficulties going on in our department, as well as cuts and uncertainties. I thought I was handling it

OK, until at the end of one day I went for a drink with one of the nurses who worked at the Health Centre where I was doing counselling – and passed out! It wasn't because I hadn't eaten or anything like that – it was just that I was really tired and not aware of it. So I have had first-hand experience of how out of touch with yourself you can get when you are so focused on helping other people.

Antonio Branco Vasco: We discussed earlier that it can be difficult for clients to be willing to ask for help if they think it's a sign of weakness. Isn't it also important for counsellors to be willing to become clients and ask for help?

Windy Dryden: I would like to think of counsellors as having a reasonable level of mental health – and if you really have problems, even for a limited time, perhaps you'd do better to take a sabbatical. But the notion that because you are a counsellor you really shouldn't, absolutely shouldn't, have problems will definitely lead you to edit them out.

I think it is realistic to accept the fact that counsellors are bound to get their fair share of human problems, and if they demand that they shouldn't, or that they should be able to cope perfectly with them, they may suffer from unfortunate consequences.

Another important point is being able to admit the limitations of your knowledge. Sometimes I'm asked questions by clients, and rather than ramble on, I say, 'Look, I don't know, but I will find out'. Similarly, I encourage trainee counsellors to share their doubts with their clients, rather than ask me questions that could easily be answered by the clients themselves.

Antonio Branco Vasco: Would you agree that one of the major strains involved in being a counsellor is the continued interaction with an atypically large number of people in need of help?

Windy Dryden: Yes. If your work consists in discussing people's problems day in and day out – in other jobs we may interact with people who have a fair share of problems, but they wouldn't necessarily talk to us about them – I think that your attention may become so focused on disturbance and dysfunction that it would probably be very healthy to go away and engage in something that gives prominence to well-being, or wellness.

Antonio Branco Vasco: Do you think that solitude and isolation have an impact on the counsellor's life?

Windy Dryden: Yes, and in this sense schools of counselling serve the important purpose of providing a sense of collegial spirit, of camaraderie, of providing meeting points where people can go to discuss problems that they are pretty sure will also be experienced by fellow counsellors – like a club!

Also perhaps 'eclectic and integrative clubs' would serve the purpose of providing a sense of belonging without the 'hardening of the categories' that some people consider happens in different schools of counselling. Whichever club we are discussing, clinicians in private practice probably need to go out of their way to attend meetings and really get a sense that they are not alone, otherwise their sense of isolation could become acute.

My own experience at the moment in Britain is that I am one of three fully trained RET practitioners in the country, and so it is difficult for us to meet up as a club! I don't mind that much because, as I was saying earlier, I have always thrived on solitude, but nevertheless I do make a yearly 'pilgrimage' to the Institute of Rational–Emotive Therapy in New York. I have done that every year since 1978, and I feel it's important to me. I also meet with counsellors from other persuasions from time to time, but I don't really get the sense of being on the same wavelength as them, although it may be nice to see them.

I think you can get some dilution of the feeling of solitude by working predominantly in groups, particularly if you have a co-leader, and counsellors who are very sociable may go out of their way to do that. But certainly you do need to guard against the effects of solitude, and participating in social activities is one of the ways of preventing burn-out.

One last observation: we have talked about deterioration in both clients and therapists – we could define burn-out as a deterioration of therapist functioning – and I think there may well be a link between the two, in that burn-out can result from not being very talented and therefore having more than your 'fair share' of failures, or from working with quite a severely disturbed population and therefore seeing less therapeutic movement than you would ideally like.

Chapter 7
Personal
Contributions

Antonio Branco Vasco: How does the fact of being a counsellor influence your life?

Windy Dryden: Well, let me begin by reiterating that I don't just practise counselling and psychotherapy. I am also an academic and a trainer of counsellors and psychotherapists. Anyway, being a counsellor influences my life first of all detrimentally. Sometimes after a hard day's work in the consulting room, I don't really want to bother with other problems. My wife may come in and want to talk to me about her day at work or friends ring me up – but I just don't want to be bothered any more.

There is an old joke about the young son of a therapist who at the end of the day wants to play with daddy or talk to daddy, but daddy – it could also be mummy – doesn't want to know, so the child says, 'How much do you charge? Can I book a session?'. This profession can definitely have a detrimental impact on relationships, and I do notice that tendency in myself; the more tired I am at the end of the day, the more I tend to edit problems out. So that's definitely a negative impact.

Antonio Branco Vasco: Does it also mean that you can't switch off from taking a therapeutic perspective on things?

Windy Dryden: Yes, although I am not quite sure whether that is an advantage or a disadvantage. Sometimes I can pick up little nuances about people's problems just from social interaction. I always feel that if only I could tell this person this or that, I might be able to help them – and sometimes I do. I don't think I would counsel them in a social setting, but I might offer them a tip or two as a friend. So perhaps a sensitivity to what somebody is saying 'beneath the surface' means that I am not quite able to enter into the social swing of things – I may be too aware of the underlying therapeutic swing of things.

On a positive note I do have a sense that I'm contributing to a worthwhile activity. Being a counsellor gives me a sense of purpose and brings meaning to my working life, and I think that's important. Helping somebody to help themselves more effectively gives me a greater sense of meaning than, say, earning an insurance company X more pounds, or making more 'widgets', or anything of that sort. This sense of meaning is probably the most important aspect of being a counsellor for me, and on balance I find my work far more rewarding than frustrating.

Antonio Branco Vasco: We seem to be going back to what you said in the first interview about how trying to make sense of your own psychological experiences led you to become interested in other people's.

Windy Dryden: Right. I think those early experiences were important. I would still prefer not to have had them, as they were quite painful, but it is a good feeling to look back and see that it wasn't all in vain. I made something of those experiences, turned them to my advantage and also helped other people as a result.

I think it is quite a powerful human tendency to want to make something meaningful out of a negative experience. I have noticed this when people talk about their experiences of cancer, loss and so on: they seem to have a powerful wish to make something good come out of it.

Antonio Branco Vasco: That reminds me of how Victor Frankl managed to create a psychotherapeutic theory out of his experience in a concentration camp. Would you like to say anything else about your work-related stresses?

Windy Dryden: Well, as I said the main stress is that at times I neglect people close to me who wish to talk, not even necessarily about their problems. In a sense I have had enough of listening. It's the same if somebody has made 'widgets' all day at work: the last thing he or she wants to do is to come home and make another 'widget'! I like to keep a fairly flexible schedule, in terms of when I see clients, but if this remains an ongoing problem I may have to introduce more structure into my life.

Anyway, I want to reiterate that I find the variety of my working life immensely rewarding. Frankly, I don't think I would like to work as a counsellor full-time. Even though each client is unique, there is clearly much more diversity between activities, such as academic work, training and clinical work, than there is within clinical work alone.

I also really value being a trainer, in that I can pass on some hard-earned lessons – but without trying to create trainees in my own image. That's something I think we need to be on guard against in our field. But variety is certainly the spice of my working life.

Antonio Branco Vasco: If you could go back to the past with the knowledge you have today and make a choice, would you still choose the same career?

Windy Dryden: Well, when my good friend Arnold Lazarus was asked that question he had to ask for clarification: do you mean if I had the same skills and talents that I have today or if I could have any skill or talent?

Antonio Branco Vasco: First, if you had the same skills and talents.

Windy Dryden: Oh yes, I would certainly choose the same career path.

Antonio Branco Vasco: And if you had other talents?

Windy Dryden: Well, if I could choose my talents I would probably choose to be a soul jazz saxophonist.

Antonio Branco Vasco: Is that related to your nickname?

Windy Dryden: Yes. I used to play a lousy saxophone, and that is why I was called Windy. But if I could play saxophone like Junior Walker, Grover Washington Jr or Kenny G, I just might be tempted to put my tenor, alto and soprano saxes on the road and peddle my wares that way. And if I could have the best of both worlds I would love to be known as the sax-playing counsellor or, to put it another way, I'd rather be a sax therapist than a sex therapist!

Antonio Branco Vasco: That reminds me of Woody Allen, because I

think your sense of humour is quite similar to his, and he plays
the clarinet very well.

Windy Dryden: Well, I am afraid I wasn't blessed with that same talent.

Antonio Branco Vasco: What do you feel about your achievements in
the field of writing?

Windy Dryden: Well, we have talked about my most important
contributions to rational–emotive therapy, but let me just
reflect on the broader question. The early 1980s were a period
of great change for me, in that I decided to take voluntary
redundancy from my job at the University of Aston and didn't
get another job for 2 years, during which, I want to add, I
received enormous supportive help from my wife, who had full
confidence in me and allowed me to structure my time as I
saw fit.

Anyway, at that time I began to feel that we in Britain were
too highly dependent on North American texts, so I decided
to edit a book called *Individual Therapy in Britain* (Dryden,
1984c), in which for the first time British experts on different
therapeutic approaches could write within a common chapter
structure, so that the foundations of a British tradition could
be laid down. That started me on something that evolved
organically rather than out of planning. I then edited two
volumes of a book called *Marital Therapy in Britain* (Dryden,
1985b,c), which developed into a series of books called
Psychotherapy in Britain, and soon afterwards I was invited to
edit a book series called *Counselling in Action*, which again
included clearly written practical guidebooks on different
therapeutic approaches, each written by a British expert. So I
think that one of the major contributions I have made has been
to encourage British writers to produce British material,
whereas before there seemed to be a lack of firm foundation
in this area. I am quite pleased with what those two series have
achieved.

Although I have edited quite a lot, I have also written quite
a lot, particularly in the area of rational–emotive therapy and
cognitive–behavioural therapy, and recently I have turned my
writing attention onto the therapeutic alliance.

My major goal has been to make my own and other people's
material available and accessible for working practitioners. I
haven't set out to write highly abstract theoretical and
complicated texts or to carry out many empircal research

studies, although I have carried out a few. My particular talent has been to write and organise other people's writings for the person who is actually working in the counselling or therapy room, and I am pleased with what I have achieved in that direction.

Making that choice has meant that it would be very difficult for me to ever get a chair or a personal professorship in Britain: I have been informally told that, no matter how many more books I write or edit, that will not be possible. I hope they are wrong, because I am reasonably ambitious in that area and I make no bones about the fact that I would like to be the first professor of counselling in Britain, but I don't think it is a realistic idea.

I am pleased, however, that I get so much feedback from counsellors and therapists who say they appreciate my efforts and value the books I have written or edited. And if I never go down in the annals of history for my contributions to counselling and psychotherapy, then that's unfortunate but, in the words of RET, hardly awful.

Antonio Branco Vasco: What are your plans for the future?

Windy Dryden: In some ways I think I have got my career round the wrong way. If I had my time over again, and if my major goal was to get a chair, I would probably involve myself in research activities and leave the editing and more clinical and theoretical writing until later. However, I am not sure whether I would have actually done that, because I don't know if my work would have made a difference. Making a difference − not necessarily a huge difference, but at least some difference for the people who are actually doing the counselling work − is very important to me.

I do have plans to do some research, although that will have to wait until I have published 50 books, since I am obsessive–compulsive and I like the order of a round number.

I have already talked about my plans for research on therapeutic failure. I may well be testing out, in the NHS Psychology Department where I work, the applicability of what is known as the '2+1' model of counselling service delivery (Dryden and Barkham, 1990).

So after I have fulfilled my writing and editing commitments I will focus more on research, and I'll have to learn to say no when people like your good self come to me and say they have a great writing or editing project! Anyway, maybe they will give me my chair when I retire. They might even give me a bath-chair!!

Antonio Branco Vasco: What do you think about contextual, cultural differences in looking at psychotherapy?

Windy Dryden: Well, I think that my writings have helped in some small way to give people in Britain a sense of 'self-reliance', a sense that we don't have to keep relying on North American texts. Whilst I think we are behind the Americans in lots of ways, there are some areas of counselling and psychotherapy in which we are international leaders – some examples are the work of the Tavistock Clinic, or the Institute of Psychiatry at the Maudsley Hospital. But at a more popular level I don't think you can have a firm sense of a British tradition if for basic texts you are relying on American material.

In the second edition of the *Psychotherapy in Britain* series we are trying to get our own back on the Americans – we are dropping the word 'Britain' from the title, because whilst we in Britain have no trouble buying American texts, they seem to have enormous trouble buying any text with the word 'Britain' in the title. So we are going to try to do a 'Trojan horse' job on them, by getting them to buy the new series which is going to be called *Psychotherapy Handbooks* and when they buy them, in their thousands hopefully, they will realise that they are reading British material, at which point it will be too late.

Antonio Branco Vasco: What advice would you give people who are starting a career as an academic or as a practitioner in the field of counselling and psychotherapy?

Windy Dryden: Let's start with the academic career. In Britain there is growing interest in counselling psychology within the British Psychological Society. I would advise younger academics not to make the mistake I made, and to get involved in research. But it is difficult to do good quality counselling research on your own; therefore, I would like to see the development of research teams, through which new academics could establish a good research tradition.

Another piece of advice would be never to stop seeing clients. It is easy to become divorced from the realities of clinical work in the groves of academia. Incidentally developing a career in counselling and psychotherapy within an academic setting is difficult, because although there is an increasing number of Masters' programmes, there are as yet no departments of counselling and psychotherapy or even, as far as I am aware, many departments of clinical psychology as distinct from general psychology departments. Therefore it may well be difficult for people in counselling and psychotherapy to get into academic positions in the numbers that I would like to see. I would like to see departments of counselling and psychotherapy set up in universities and polytechnics. So in summary my advice would be involve yourself in research activities *and* keep relevant by continuing to see clients.

As for people who are considering a career in counselling, I would advise them to give some thought to why they want to get into this profession. Counselling is now an 'in' activity, so lots of courses are being set up and are enrolling a good many students – although I don't know how many of them end up actually practising. I think it is very important to become aware of your motives, and there are books like the one I edited with a colleague *On Becoming a Psychotherapist* (Dryden and Spurling, 1989) which could be quite helpful for people to read as a stimulus to this kind of exploration.

Other things to do in preparation for training include hunting around for the most appropriate course, involving yourself in some helping activities – though not necessarily counselling – to see what it feels like, and experiencing some counselling for yourself to have a taste of what being a client means.

I find it amazing that many of the people who apply for my Master's course in counselling at Goldsmiths' College haven't read anything about counselling! Reading some of the literature can help you to make an informed decision about counselling as a career. I don't think it's enough to say at an interview 'My friends tell me I am a good listener' – that's important, but there are other dimensions.

Another point worth bearing in mind is that, whatever course you choose, it will certainly be demanding, and it may well lead to some degree of personal upheaval. Therefore it is important to talk it over with major significant others and alert them to the fact that this might be the case. If you have a wife or husband, it might be worth while to go into some form of couple counselling just to talk about the impact of training. Over the years I have seen a number of marriages or partnerships break up as a result of one person going into training.

People should also realise that, as the situation stands at the moment in Britain, they will not earn that much money, and there isn't a career structure yet for counsellors and psychotherapists, although that may well change in the future. Clinical psychologists have a career structure but counsellors and psychotherapists don't.

Antonio Branco Vasco: What advice would you give someone concerning when to begin training as a counsellor?

Windy Dryden: I think it may be a good idea to hold off until around age 25 or 26 before starting training. Having said that, I started training when I was 24, so don't do as I do, do as I say!! But I think that training in counselling and psychotherapy does need some maturity. If you are coming straight from an undergraduate degree course, unless you are very unusual, you are probably not ready yet.

Overall, there should be awareness that this is an arduous profession, although a very rewarding one.

Antonio Branco Vasco: Isn't it also important to be aware of your vision of reality and how it relates to your chosen theoretical orientation?

Windy Dryden: Know yourself, know what kind of vision of reality or epistemology you hold dear. See that there is a creative match between those types of issues and the type of training that you are seeking. So, yes, I think you are right there. Not only know thyself but know thy vision of reality, thy epistemology and ontology. So I can imagine when I next interview somebody for my Master's course in counselling I will say, 'Please sit down and tell me all about your epistemology, vision of reality and ontology'!!!

Antonio Branco Vasco: Thank you, Windy.

References

BORDIN, E. (1979). The generalizability of the psychoanalytic concept of the working alliance. *Psychotherapy: Theory, Research and Practice*, **16**, 252–260.

CLARK, D.M. (1986). A cognitive approach to panic. *Behaviour Research and Therapy*, **24**, 461–470.

CORNSWEET, C. (1983). Nonspecific factors and theoretical choice. *Psychotherapy: Theory, Research and Practice*, **20**, 307–313.

DEVINE, D.A. and FERNALD, P.S. (1973). Outcome effects of receiving a preferred, randomly assigned or non-preferred therapy. *Journal of Consulting and Clinical Psychology*, **41**, 104–107.

DRYDEN, W. (1984a). Therapeutic arenas. In: W. Dryden (Ed.), *Individual Therapy in Britain*. Milton Keynes: Open University Press.

DRYDEN, W. (1984b). Rational–emotive therapy. In: W. Dryden (Ed.), *Individual therapy in Britain*. Milton Keynes: Open University Press.

DRYDEN, W. (Ed.) (1984c). *Individual therapy in Britain*. Milton Keynes: Open University Press.

DRYDEN, W. (1985a). Marital therapy: The rational–emotive approach. In: W. Dryden (Ed.), *Marital Therapy in Britain, Vol. 1: Context and therapeutic approaches*. Milton Keynes: Open University Press.

DRYDEN, W. (Ed.) (1985b). *Marital Therapy in Britain. Vol. 1: Context and therapeutic approaches*. Milton Keynes: Open University Press.

DRYDEN, W. (Ed.) (1985c). *Marital Therapy in Britain. Vol 2: Special areas*. Milton Keynes: Open University Press.

DRYDEN, W. (1986). Eclectic psychotherapies: A critique of leading approaches. In: J.C. Norcross (Ed.), *Handbook of Eclectic Psychotherapy*. New York: Brunner/Mazel.

DRYDEN, W. (1987). Theoretically consistent eclecticism: Humanizing a computer 'addict'. In J.C. Norcross (Ed.), *Casebook of Eclectic Psychotherapy*. New York: Brunner/Mazel.

DRYDEN, W. and BARKHAM, M. (1990). The two-plus one model: A dialogue. *Counselling Psychology Review*, **5**(4), 5–18.

DRYDEN, W. and DIGIUSEPPE, R. (1990). *A Primer on Rational–Emotive Therapy*. Champaign, IL: Research Press.

DRYDEN, W. and SPURLING, L. (Eds) (1989). *On Becoming a Psychotherapist*. London: Routledge.

ELLIS, A. (1987). Integrative developments in rational-emotive therapy (RET). *Journal of Integrative and Eclectic Psychotherapy*, **6**, 470–479.

ELLIS, A. and HARPER, R. (1975). *A New Guide to Rational Living.* N. Hollywood, CA: Wilshire.

EYSENCK, H.J. (1990). *Rebel with a Cause.* London: W.H. Allen.

GRUNEBAUM, H. (1986). Harmful psychotherapy experience. *American Journal of Psychotherapy*, 40, 165–176.

HART, J. (1986). Functional eclectic therapy. In: J.C. Norcross (Ed.), *Handbook of Eclectic Psychotherapy.* New York: Brunner/Mazel.

LAZARUS, A.A. (1989). *The Practice of Multimodal Therapy.* Baltimore, MD: John Hopkins Press.

LAZARUS, A.A. (1990). Why I am an eclectic (not an integrationist). In: W. Dryden and J.C. Norcross (Eds), *Eclecticism and Integration in Counselling and Psychotherapy.* Loughton, Essex: Gale Centre Publications.

MAHONEY, M.J. (1986). The tyranny of technique. *Counseling and Values*, 30, 169–174.

MALUCCIO, A.N. (1979). *Learning from Clients: Interpersonal helping as viewed by clients and social workers.* New York: Free Press.

MASSON, J.M. (1988). *Against Therapy.* New York: Atheneum.

MESSER, S.B. (1990). Integration and eclecticism in counselling and psychotherapy: Cautionary notes. In: W. Dryden and J.C. Norcross (Eds), *Eclecticism and Integration in Counselling and Psychotherapy.* Loughton, Essex: Gale Centre Publications.

NORCROSS, J.C. (Ed.) (1986). *Handbook of Eclectic Psychotherapy.* New York: Brunner/Mazel.

PROCHASKA, J.O. and DICLEMENTE, C.L. (1986). The transtheoretical approach. In: J.C. Norcross (Ed.), *Handbook of Eclectic Psychotherapy.* New York: Brunner/Mazel.

STAATS, A. (1983). *Psychology: The crisis of disunity.* New York: Praeger.

Index

2196874